"After 20 years of listening to women about their most personal life and health issues, I have learned they want authenticity and transparency. Julie's book is just that; it is an honest, raw account of her rise to success. She is unafraid to take on the topics of work life balance, the pressures of being a working mother, and ageism in the industry. She does so in an approachable, disarming manner, with a sprinkle of her trademark humor. In an era of endless self help books, Julie offers the advice you have always desired, but no one has dared to deliver."

Dr. Somi Javaid
Founder & CMO, HerMD

"Fabulous!!! When Julie walks into a room the fun begins. Julie and I both have Louisiana roots, so it is probably the Cajun/Zydeco music and the crayfish and gumbo that makes us kindred spirits. Julie went to LSU; but LSU denied me entry in 1961, because of my race. I'm Black. The difference is that I didn't possess Julie's 'boldness.' Julie would have knocked LSU's doors down and made them explain why they were trying to keep her out of her state's university. Boldness takes the mask off the bad guys. They can't stand up to the scrutiny of the bold examiner. If only I had known Julie and had her by my side throughout my career. This book puts her spirit by your side to bring out the boldness you need for happiness in your life."

Edwin Rigaud
Chairman & Owner, EnovaPremier
Former VP of Food & Beverage, Procter and Gamble
Former President & CEO, National
Underground Railroad Freedom Center

"I have had the privilege of seeing this absolute rock star in action, and learning from her directly! What an influence on my life! From the moment I met Julie, she took me under her wing, constantly emboldening and empowering me to be the best I could be professionally and personally. How exciting that her fascinating and insightful stories, with so much wisdom woven through them, are now out there for the world! I can think of no one better to inspire boldness and meaningful change in your life."

Sina Gebre-Ab
News Anchor, WJZ-TV Baltimore

"Knowing Julie, she personifies BOLDNESS in all the positive ways. She figured out early that BOLDNESS done well is endearing and contagious. Through her poignant and honest writing, women and men alike will learn that boldness doesn't mean being a bulldozer or never messing up. It means embracing the successes and failures, and trials and errors, with a good dose of humor, making everyone around you so comfortable with your boldness that they, too, become BOLD."

Nancy Aichholz
Founder & CEO, That's So Sweet
Nationally recognized mentor/coach for female founders

"I had spent 22 years in the 'bigs,' including five years as a New York based network correspondent, when I rolled into Baton Rouge to work for fun. There I encountered a lot of young starters in the business. And then along came this phenomenal talent with a musical laugh and calculating drive that came from more than 'just another pretty face.' Julie O'Neill was a hard driving reporter who taught me a thing or two. Me! Mr. Hot Shot anchor who had cornered annual salaries just south of a million dollars. Julie. Bold but not brash. Bold but bucolic. And I loved her work every step of the way. In the book, Julie draws the distinction between 'being bold' and the male mantra of 'growing a set.' They're similar. Julie's guides bring more success."

George Sells
Legendary News Anchor/Reporter of 50+ years

"As the proud mother of a Special Forces Green Beret, I know what boldness in action is like. My son's combat injuries in service to his country, which eventually led to his death, inspired me to establish the Greater Cincinnati Chapter of the Green Beret Foundation. Through her reporting, I watched Julie work tirelessly on and off the air to bring the plight of our valiant Green Berets and their families into the forefront. Through her volunteer efforts, I have seen Julie's heart and compassion for the service of our military. This is a woman who knows boldness, and this book captures it, a gift to all."

Fran Wesseling
Green Beret Foundation National Board Member

"I worked side by side with Julie for years as her producer at a news station in Cincinnati. We were an incredible team! And our relationship blossomed over dinner breaks, during which we'd hash out all things work and life. I had a front row seat watching how she found a way to pave a path around every one of life's obstacles, always coming out on top. Julie O'Neill knows boldness. I'm betting you're going to love this book, because I would never bet against Julie."

Griffin Frank
Cable network news producer

BOLD

The Secret To My BIG WINS
To Help YOU
CRASH Through Your Comfort Zone

JULIE O'NEILL

Cover picture: Little Rascals Photography

Library of Congress Control Number: 2023904274

ISBN: 979-8-9876638-0-6 (paperback)
ISBN: 979-8-9876638-1-3 (ebook)

To my mother, the boldest human being I know.

Freedom lies in being bold.

Robert Frost

CONTENTS

INTRODUCTION

You gotta listen to your girlfriends' advice, however it might make you uncomfortable. They know stuff. They know you. They're your own personal Board of Directors.

Several months ago, a couple of my best girlfriends who sit in top floor offices met me for a power lunch to talk strategy. I asked them to weigh in on what they need at their companies.

"What would help you?" I asked.

One quickly put a fork full of caesar salad down onto her plate, and took a few moments with her head in her hand, to really think about my question. Then her answer came.

"I need women to bring more boldness to the workplace, so they can move up and wield more influence in the big decisions," she said. "Women have so much value to give, but too many are not doing what it takes to bring that value."

My other girlfriend gave a nod of approval.

Then as I launched into what I would include in this book on being bold, both forks came down as each sat up in her chair to chime in.

It was energizing.

In the minutes that followed, sitting around the back corner table at Stone Creek Restaurant in Montgomery, Ohio, I got tremendous feedback, and a clear directive from these two members of my "Board."

"Julie, you're going to have to go all the way here," they said. "A book about the importance of being bold won't amount to a hill of beans, unless you spill the beans. Tell your poignant and funny tales of adventure, and share your insights," they said.

"But you also have to reeeeally get real, and talk about what people don't talk about," both agreed. "You have to flip on the floodlight to show people what lurks in the dark. What happened to you. What happens to so many women, and yes some men too, when they reach a certain age. You have to practice boldness as you're preaching it," they insisted.

It was the resounding consensus as I hosted more brainstorming sessions with other men and women of my inner circle in the weeks that followed.

I sincerely hope you'll have fun reading about the fantastic, magical career I had, bringing boldness to TV news. It might surprise you what goes on behind the scenes.

Even more, though, it's my great wish that you glean something meaningful that will bring more boldness to your life and career, especially as I open up about experiences it brings me no pleasure to share. My girlfriends weren't wrong. It has to be said.

CHAPTER 1

UNDER THE BIG TOP

Fun for all ages, Come Join the Thrills

Every family has its own "Big Top," under which we grow up juggling, jumping from platforms, and clowning around to figure out how we fit into the show. If we are lucky enough to have a family that caught us when we fell from a trapeze, we venture out into the world with a sense of self and a sense of security.

I was blessed to have such a family. Before I take you out onto the high wire and make my case for bringing boldness to your life and career, I'll give you a little background on who and what propped me up to that wire, for my 30 year act as "that news lady."

I was born in the midst of one of New York City's worst blizzards. My parents had moved from Baton Rouge to the Big Apple, so Dad could pursue a career as an opera singer. MawMaw and PawPaw Ragusa (my grandparents on my mother's side) flew up to New York in the middle of the big storm and trudged through the snow and ice to arrive at the hospital just after my birth.

As the story goes, my exhausted grandmother somehow found the strength to make a b-line to the nurses' station, to ask if the O'Neill baby had been born yet.

"Yes," a nurse answered.

MawMaw took a breath, still bundled up in her coat and shivering from the cold, and asked, "Could you tell me if it's a boy or a girl?"

"She had a baby girl," the nurse answered.

MawMaw leaned in. "Are you sure?" She persisted.

"Yes, I'm sure," the nurse answered.

Then MawMaw found her way to a bench in an empty hallway of the hospital, put her head down into her hands, and cried tears of joy.

MawMaw was a seamstress and hadn't had a little girl to make a dress for since my mother. After Mom came two sons and four grandsons. She finally had a granddaughter.

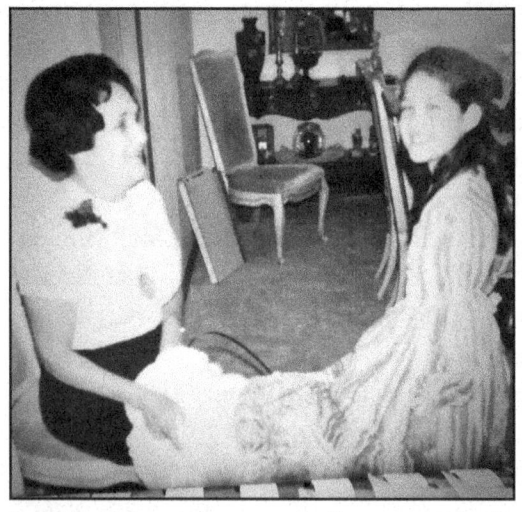

MawMaw Josie Ragusa, a seamstress, fits young Julie for a dress.

I start with this story because it captures so well how loved and valued I was, as I grew up the first granddaughter in a big family of dynamic and captivating performers, one more bold than the next. P.T. Barnum would've loved a front row seat to my show.

At the time I was born, my dad was singing at "the Met" and other well known venues In New York City. He had a regular gig as the lead tenor at the church pastored by Dr. Norman Vincent Peale, author of *The Power of Positive Thinking*, a long time New York Times Bestseller. Dr. Peale had a great influence on my dad, who reminded me throughout my childhood to be careful of what I think and say, because our thoughts and words determine our success and happiness.

Jack and Jo E. O'Neill

Jack and Jo E. (Dad and Mom) had moved away from Baton Rouge right after tying the knot to take the world by storm. She was the smart, savvy beauty queen and he was the talented charmer who'd give her a life of adventure. They met as my father was playing in a golf tournament. In addition to being a singer, he was a scratch golfer, and was the youngest golfer ever to win the Men's Golf City Championship in Baton Rouge, at just 16 years old. In high school, he'd skip class and jump the fence at a course near his home to drive, chip, and putt golf balls all day.

My mother had her own escapades in high school, namely sneaking off to "take off" with her boyfriend, who'd gotten his pilot license at sixteen. That pilot boyfriend was none other than Barry Seal, the infamous drug smuggler portrayed by Tom Cruise in the movie *American Made*. For the record, the illegal activity started way after my mother dated him in their teen years, but you get the idea that I got the risk-taker gene from both Mom and Dad.

My parents also had a strong faith and strong sense of family. By my fifth birthday, Mom was taking care of three children living in our Staten Island home, while Dad was riding the ferry to sing wherever he could get work in "the city." It felt like the right time to head back to Baton Rouge, help run the family piano business, "O'Neill's Music House," and raise the kids closer to the family.

In my family's circus, any of the men could be "the Strong Man," but PawPaw Ragusa definitely ran the show as the ringmaster. Being full Italian, he was jokingly nicknamed "The Godfather" by his friends. Though very personable, he could be a force when it came to something he felt strongly about.

As a young boy in grade school, PawPaw wanted to have a middle name, not having received one at birth. He decided he liked the name "Young" and started turning in his school papers with "Joseph Young Ragusa" written at the top. His teacher wasn't having it. She quickly reminded him he was Catholic, and told him "Young" was not appropriate because it was a Mormon name. He kept on including "Young." The teacher told him if he didn't stop, she'd give him a zero in the class. PawPaw took the zero. And it didn't end there. As an adult, he legally added "Young" as his middle name, and then named his first born son "Brigham Young." Uncle Brigham, my godfather, loves to tell the story to his fellow Catholic friends.

*The Ragusa and O'Neill bunch gathers for
annual Easter volleyball game.*

The whole big Italian family—aunts, uncles and cousins—converged on PawPaw and MawMaw Ragusa's house on Sunday afternoons following Mass. We were a raucous bunch, one personality bigger than the next. After spaghetti lunch, the adults retired to the living room to swap opinions and stories, while the cousins retreated to the yard with a milk carton for a competitive game of "kick the can." Any tensions that arose got snuffed out swiftly and sternly. We were to mend ways and move on. One of PawPaw's famous lines was, "I can't make you do it, but I can make you wish you had."

Even after the passing of our patriarch and matriarch, we all still gather on Christmas Eve night at my mother's house to eat biscuits, eggs and sausage (reminiscent of LSU post-game gatherings) and sing Christmas carols. Understand that most of the bunch on Mom's side doesn't sing a note all year. They just love cutting up, and wouldn't miss "The 12 Days of Christmas," in which everyone is assigned a "day" to sing.

Dad's side of the family had the musical talent. Gampa O'Neill was a concert pianist. Gamma O'Neill, my dad and Aunt Patt, were opera singers. The grandkids all sang mostly for fun. My older brother Raph will never live down our *Donny and Marie* act at the St. George Elementary School Talent Night, where we all attended grade school. My sister Laurie's big moment came playing the lead role in *Oklahoma* at St. Joseph's Academy, the all girls Catholic high school we both attended. I always

Raph & Julie O'Neill perform Donny & Marie act for St. George Elementary School Talent Night.

went for the character roles, my favorite being "The Queen" in *Once Upon a Mattress*.

All of us performed in *The O'Neill Family Christmas Show*, which aired on local television. One year as we were doing the show live on Christmas Day, we ended up with extra time to fill at the end of the show, which led to my first impromptu live performance.

My mother in a panic turned to me, her six-year-old, and said, "Julie, would you like to play a song on the piano?" She'll tell you I boldly walked over to the piano without hesitation, but the video shows a hint of consternation on my face as I plunked out "Silent Night." Then came a big smile (missing two front teeth) at my relief that I made it through without a mistake.

*Julie (age 6) plays "Silent Night" during live
O'Neill Family Christmas Show on WAFB-TV
in Baton Rouge. (Courtesy WAFB-TV)*

I often wonder what was going on in my young brain in those moments. I have to believe the synapses were firing by the end when I reached success. It was good to be the family hero in the clutch that day.

It came as no surprise to anyone that I chose to study voice in college. My freshman year, I went to Centenary College in Shreveport, Louisiana and had the adventure of my life taking an around-the-world tour with the choir.

Japan. China. Thailand. India. Then England.

While in Agra, India, my friend Heather and I snuck off from the rest of the group to take a camel ride to the Taj Mahal. I suppose I can admit to that now. There we were trodding along through a village on the other side of the world atop a camel that labored like it was close to death. Crazy 19-year-olds. Mostly that trip gave me a cultural worldview, which would forever influence

*Julie and friend Heather
take a camel ride to the
Taj Mahal in Agra,
India (1987).*

my sense of gratitude and responsibility that I was born in the U.S.A.

I left Centenary College in favor of studying "psychology" for a year at Louisiana State University (LSU). Then quickly flipped back to pursuing the stage, with my high school friend Ana urging me to join her at the prestigious College Conservatory of Music (CCM) at the University of Cincinnati. "You gotta get up here," she insisted. She sold me, but there was the matter of getting accepted.

When I called the head of the musical theater program, he was emphatic that auditions were closed and he already had too many students. I pestered him with phone calls for weeks, pleading, "If I fly to Cincinnati, will you just hear me sing?" He finally acquiesced. And yes, I got in.

I spent a year at CCM and then did my first and only professional show the summer after, playing Edwin Drood in *The Mystery of Edwin Drood* at a small outdoor theater in Prestonsburg, Kentucky. Doing the role was electrifying, but living in an old trailer with mice as roommates, not so much. It was time to go home and rethink my career choice, yet again.

It was my mother who brought up the idea of reporting for TV news, always an admirer of my writing. She's quite the writer herself when properly fired up. Mom worked as a legal secretary, so she knows how to churn out a scathing rebuke with the proper formality, which makes her letters all the more intimidating. She's not the type to flinch at anything that needs addressing, even known to get out of her car and direct traffic. And we started calling her "MacGyver Mom" years ago because she can build or fix anything, always working on some project.

One important project for both of my parents was to get me settled on how I was going to make a living. At Mom's suggestion, I decided to jump into the ring of broadcast journalism, enrolling again at LSU.

Who knew what a circus TV news would be? Perfect for me. As you'll see in the chapters ahead, it offered all the daring feats and high wire acts of the Big Top I grew up under.

CHAPTER 2

KATY BAR THE DOOR

How I Broke Into Broadcast News

If you're looking for a shortcut, think like a criminal. That's the long and short of how I "broke into" the exclusive club of broadcast news.

No I'm not suggesting I violated any laws, just that channeling a little crafty ingenuity to get around the rules in place for entering my profession made perfect sense for me. There were 100-thousand students graduating in broadcast journalism that year, with just two thousand entry level positions open, according to one of my college professors. Not encouraging news for a girl aspiring to be a working journalist.

As often happens in life, my big opportunity to get my foot in the door came just as I had another door slammed in my face.

The summer before my sixth year of college (yep 6 years!), the grand plan was to win the Miss America pageant. I had switched majors and universities several times and now I knew exactly the path I would take to make my mark on the world. World peace? No problem. I had won the Miss Baton Rouge pageant a few years before and made it to the top 10 at Miss Louisiana, even winning the talent competition as an 18-year-old. Now I was 21, much more mature and knew exactly what to do to win the crown. Oh to have the self-assurance of a 21-year-old woman at her power weight!

Let me say this: It's ok to be shamelessly idealistic at 21. That wide-eyed girl still drives many of my big decisions today.

Julie wins "Miss Baton Rouge" pageant.
(Photo by John Bonfanti, 1986)

Anyhow, so sure that this was my destiny, I started my summer internship at my hometown station, WAFB-TV, somewhat half-heartedly. I let the staff know from the get-go I would be gone for a week in June to compete in Miss Louisiana. Before I left the building for that week off, I proudly reminded the anchors, reporters, producers and all to watch the pageant airing on state-wide television that next Saturday night.

It never occurred to me I wouldn't make it to the top 10. But that's exactly what happened. I remember like yesterday standing there on stage after the tenth name was called out and it wasn't mine. The audience applauded. The music played. The emcee congratulated the finalists. And there I stood. Frozen. Mortified. Devastated. No one watching from home would hear me sing my song, model my swimsuit, or answer a question in my evening gown. Instead all those people I'd told to watch would only see me exit stage left with the other girls who didn't make the cut.

Go ahead, snicker and roll your eyes at the dreamy-eyed pageant girl with grandiose visions of greatness, based on a contest that incorporated duct tape to hold up breasts and sticky spray to tack down a swimsuit. I shake my head at that now, too. But at the time I was swallowed up in the humiliation and feelings of worthlessness. I felt so embarrassed that I had done so poorly, so publicly. So ashamed that I had let everybody down. Most of all, my dream was dead. And I felt dead inside.

In retrospect, I know how valuable it's been for a Type A competitor like me to lose big from time to time. Winning feels good, but it does little to feed a person's sense of compassion for others, a critical quality in order to have meaningful relationships. That's what I tell myself in failure.

Losing still stinks in the moment though.

The idea of walking into the TV station to continue my internship the next week felt like a fate worse than death. But there was no getting out of it. I grew up in an era that was barren of wallowing. I can still hear my mother's shouts from the kitchen any day I want to stay in bed.

"Get up Julie Catherine! If you miss that bus, you're walking to school!"

Of course it felt a little easier to face the staff at WAFB with each passing day. Time heals, especially when we turn our attention to something else. And wonder of wonders, no one at the station cared. Nobody was thinking about me or any contest. They were more concerned about their own problems. People always are.

Within a couple of weeks, it was *what pageant?* I was having the summer of my life. I'd go with this reporter named Marsanne Golsby to the State Capitol and help pick the soundbites from her interviews with legislators. (A soundbite is the portion of an interview that gets picked to air on the news.) Marsanne was a force. A smart, savvy investigative reporter. She'd get it done like a bull in a china shop if that's what it took. No nonsense. No apologies. She took me under her wing. I'll never forget Marsanne telling me one day I had a good ear for soundbites.

At some point I got to go out into the field without Marsanne, just me with a photographer to get MOS's (man on the street interviews) for a new segment created by the assistant news director, Liz Golson Combs. It was called The People Factor. Each Friday evening the station would have viewers weigh in on a different topic, like their favorite ice cream or what they liked for breakfast. It was strictly fluff and fun, but it engaged viewers, which Liz knew how to do long before social media came onto the scene. A few years later under her direction, this mid-sized market television station's late night newscasts (featuring the legendary George Sells and the late great Donna Britt) would boast the second highest ratings in the nation.

Former WAFB-TV main anchors Donna Britt
and George Sells (Courtesy WAFB-TV)

Liz reached out to me on social media a couple of years ago. We messaged back and forth, exchanging cell phone numbers with the promise we'd talk soon. Sadly, she died of a longtime sickness before that phone call happened. Had I only known. Lesson learned. Slow down and make time for old friends. You never know what they might be going through.

My exciting summer of shadowing reporters and grabbing soundbites passed swiftly. As the internship was coming to a close and I was preparing to return to the grind of getting college wrapped up, something absolutely unexpected and unheard of happened. Marsanne and Liz told me I should try to stay on at the station, as a paid reporter.

What? I thought.

You're suggesting I try to get hired?

Now?

I've mentioned my college professor's warning that the odds of getting hired didn't bode well for journalism graduates. And I still had a year to go to get my college degree. Plus, I certainly did not have the mandatory 2 years of experience necessary to be considered for a job in the 93rd TV Market that was Baton Rouge. *Why would these two news women think I could get hired now?*

It's no small gift to believe in someone.

The power it gave me as a 21-year-old, who was dying of shame and embarrassment at the loss of that pageant not two months prior, was immeasurable.

I went home with a fantastic feeling of wonder. *Why not*, I thought. *I can talk my way into a reporting job.*

Suddenly, the belief these two women had in me had the wheels in my head firing on all cylinders. Sparks were flying. An idea came from nowhere. Then more ideas followed. I was figuring out what I would say to assure every excuse the news director could possibly come up with to shoot down my pitch would be trumped by an obvious reason to bring me on board.

All dutiful preparation aside, when the time came to deliver my spiel to the news director at WAFB, I was a nervous wreck. Nick Simonette was and is a super kind, cool guy, but back then as a young woman my authority figure issues were in full swing. I still shudder when I think of how it felt to even walk up to him and speak to him. It didn't matter how friendly he was. In my mind he was all powerful and I was nothing, and that made him very intimidating.

How am I going to calm my nerves and convince this man I'm a confident woman? I thought.

This was going to require boldness.

Having or conjuring boldness means different things to different people in different circumstances.

Merriam-Webster defines "bold" as "showing or requiring a fearless daring spirit."[1]

For the purposes of this book, I'm focused more on our capacity as people to *show* boldness, even if we're enveloped in fear.

Boldness does not require actual confidence or authentic belief in oneself. It does not require age or experience. It's strictly a mindset. It's something one can grab ahold of like one would a briefcase and take into a meeting or any situation.

The good news about boldness is— because it's a mindset, you can "fake it" in order to feel it.

> *Boldness does not require actual confidence or authentic belief in oneself. It does not require age or experience. It's strictly a mindset.*

I've learned through the years the "fake it till you make it" phenomenon is invaluable. There's tremendous neuroscientific research on this. One of the great pearls I uncovered came from a psychotherapist named Hilary Jacobs Hendel. She wrote an article entitled, "The Role of Make Believe Play in Adult Life." (Hendel, 2016) In it she says it's a scientific fact: "The brain cannot tell the difference between fantasy and reality."[2]

Take that in for a moment. We've been told that thinking about ocean waves rolling onto a beach can bring down our heart rate. We don't actually have to be in our happy place. We just have to think about our happy place in order to physically change our bodies. In her article Hendel very succinctly explains why pretending, or "faking it," changes us: the brain doesn't know the difference.

I would offer to you then, that the capacity to be bold requires nothing more than pretending you have the capacity to be bold. True confidence necessitates actual previous success and develops with each victory, but boldness requires only a mindset, and it'll do while your self-confidence is still under construction.

So here I was sitting in Nick Simonette's office, the most powerful person in the world. (That's any person who currently has what you want most.) I pitched my idea.

Nick should hire me to do one segment per week. I would put together, on tape, all of the questions and answers involved in "The People Factor" segment.

Having "The People Factor" all on one tape to slide into the machine would make the show easier to direct than the current process of switching back and forth between the anchors and soundbites.

I would be the perfect reporter for this, being such a "people person," I told Nick.

Hiring me would put a fresh new face on the air, and it would also mean having another person in the newsroom to answer phones and help develop other stories.

Having me as an employee would also help the team break more stories, since I had such a large extended family with lots of local contacts.

And since the segment would be taped, Nick could check my work for quality before it aired on TV so there would be no risk of embarrassment to the station.

Notice my pitch came with solutions to problems for Nick. Solutions are the foundation of any good pitch. Let them know how you're going to make their life easier. The more solutions the better.

As I took a breath to let Nick respond, I first received with relief a nice long smile. It was a warm smile that permeated a parent's pride. It said, *Look at this little intern with her big idea. Good for her.* Then, shifting in his seat, his countenance changing a bit, his words came, announcing the other problem that was going to be the missile that shot this whole thing out of the sky.

"We don't have an opening for a reporter right now and there is no money in the budget to create even a part-time opening," he said.

Nick had to have expected to see my face drop in despondence. It didn't.

What he saw was the look of eager anticipation. A sparkle in my eye.

He had set me up so beautifully to deliver the most brilliant part of my pitch, which I had intentionally held back.

As he delivered what he thought would be the defeating blow, it was like that moment in one of my middle school volleyball games when the crowd's eyes followed the ball I'd just set up so perfectly, and everyone braced as they watched

Suzanne Cafferel's feet spring up from the gym room floor, her arm flying overhead to spike the ball over the net. Suzanne was a superstar athlete. The great lob was now coming in this meeting with Nick, and this time I got to spike it.

"Well Nick, here's what I'm thinking," I said with a smile creeping up the side of my mouth. "You won't hire me as a reporter and put me on the clock. You'll contract me to do just this segment, and my fee is $20 per segment."

Nick leaned in.

I continued on.

"It doesn't matter how long it takes me to get this segment done. It will cost you only 20 dollars a week," I said.

Then I shut up. This is a key component in any negotiation, letting the moment resonate and sink in. I'm not sure how I knew to do this or was able to do this at this moment, because friends know shutting up has never come naturally to me.

Nick stayed quiet for a moment too.

Then his eyebrows lifted, revealing his obvious intrigue.

And then came the words, "Well, I'll have to take that proposal upstairs."

"Upstairs" is where the general manager's office was. Our meeting ended with the understanding that the news director of WAFB-TV was going to go up to his boss's office and pitch this idea to hire me.

Woo hoo!

It didn't take long, a day or two, before I had the answer. I was in. I was "The People Factor" reporter.

Within a month of doing my taped segment, I was tossing to it live on the news set. I remember sitting on the set for the first time, pretending I was Connie Chung, the first lady of TV news back then. That would get me through my nervousness, as I navigated the camera changes, the teleprompter, and the producer talking to me through an earpiece.

Julie delivers "People Factor" report on set with then WAFB anchor Nancy Parker in 1991. (Courtesy WAFB-TV)

The old "fake it till you make it" trick helped calm me enough to get through the first live TV experience, and I got smoother each week.

A couple of months after coming on board as "The People Factor" reporter, a weekend spot opened up and Nick gave me my shot at being a bonafide TV news reporter.

"I need to know that you can do this, and you're not going to be coming to me with a million questions," I remember Nick saying.

"Oh, don't worry, I can do this," I assured him. I didn't really know I could do it. Frankly, I didn't know how to do it, but that's what you have to say. And after weeks and months of stressing over how to boil down interviews and information into a one minute and 30 second news story, sweating every deadline, I did finally start to figure it out.

I was a rising reporter.

And within one year of starting my summer internship at WAFB, which was one week after I graduated from LSU with a degree in Broadcast Journalism…

wait for it…

I was ANCHORING THE STATION'S MORNING SHOW!

Julie anchors WAFB morning show in 1992. (Courtesy WAFB-TV)

That's what you call a meteoric rise.

———◇———

Telling the story of my genesis into journalism has been a regular indulgence for me over the decades since. I especially love sharing it with the young people I mentor, trying to figure out how to get their foot in the door of the profession they're pursuing.

We all have stories we like to tell, or at least like to think back on, and with good reason. Reliving successes sends that happy signal to the brain as though you're eating that spoonful of Graeter's Raspberry Chocolate Chip ice cream all over again.

Oh yes indeed!
Good stuff!
We need this.

Reliving our glories helps set our confidence markers into stone. These are life moments that give us powerful positive reinforcement.

Reliving our glories helps set our confidence markers into stone. These are life moments that give us powerful positive reinforcement.

I want you to really lean into this if there is an area in which you are lacking the confidence you need to crash through your comfort zone and go get what you want.

Consider how a young college student with no training or experience landed a job in the extremely competitive TV news business, without even putting together a video resume.

It was a confluence of three things.

First, someone else's belief that this was possible sparked my belief that this was possible. You must, must, must believe.

Second, I got myself connected to my creativity, to craft a plan to sell myself to this boss. God gives everyone creative impulses, that each of us can tap into by tuning in and listening. You must tune into and trust your creativity.

Third, I was willing to be bold when I had no right to be. Anybody can find a way to "break into" the place they want to be, especially someone with a criminal mind.

CHAPTER 3

THEN ALONG CAME BILL

The Day I Spilled Coffee on a Future President

There's something to be said about having doggedness when you don't know any better. It's a cousin to boldness and a necessity in the up and coming years of building a career, certainly in the news biz.

I was just a few months into my journalism career, reporting part-time on weekends for WAFB in Baton Rouge in 1992, when I got a call from the president of the Baton Rouge Jaycees. The Jaycees had sponsored the Miss Baton Rouge pageant in previous years, which I'd won now five years earlier. The club's president was proud to see his queen on TV. Apparently he had something to do with former President Bill Clinton's first campaign for the White House, because that's what he was calling about.

"I have a tip for you, Julie," he said. "I know where Bill Clinton is going to be and how you can try to get a one-on-one interview with him before his news conference in town Saturday afternoon."

Who's Bill Clinton? I thought.

Ok, don't think too poorly of me. I was still a full-time college student. Between school and working weekends, it was tough to keep up with the news. At that time, Clinton was the governor of Arkansas running second in the polls for the Democratic nomination.

I remember thinking the name Clinton sounded familiar, but I couldn't place it.

"Uh huh," I answered my old friend, as panic set in. I didn't want to lose all credibility and embarrass myself forever by asking who Bill Clinton was.

Let me say something here that lent itself very useful to me, growing up in a business in which you're expected to know a lot of stuff, and your mistakes and bad moments are often on TV for the world to see.

I had to learn how to shake off my fear of embarrassment. That fear got in the way of asking important questions. And when I allowed myself to get tortured over embarrassing moments, that got in the way of my ability to move forward and perform well on the next thing in front of me.

As in any relationship, your compatibility with embarrassment can improve over time with deliberate intention. Somewhere along the line I stumbled upon a trick I wasn't even aware I was using to ease the malaise of humiliating moments. After I'd say or do something stupid or otherwise cringe-worthy, I'd laugh and say, "Good thing I don't embarrass easily." Sometimes I said it out loud. Sometimes I just said it to myself.

Once I was having lunch with a boss I wanted to impress. A woman from across the restaurant waved. I waved back with a smile, thinking this woman must recognize me from TV. Just my luck, she was waving at someone behind me. Ugh!

My boss couldn't help but chuckle and poke fun at me. I immediately threw my hands up, rolled my eyes and said with a smile, "Good thing I don't embarrass easily." It diffused the whole awkward moment. And I could let it go.

This is one little trick I use to achieve something critically important. If you want to bring boldness to what you do, you have to free yourself from the bondage of the fear of embarrassment.

If you want to bring boldness to what you do, you have to free yourself from the bondage of the fear of embarrassment.

In my early days of reporting, I was still too scared to ask the embarrassing question, so I listened for context clues as the conversation continued with the head of the Jaycees.

"I know he's trailing for the Democratic nomination right now, Julie, but I really think he's going to be our next president," he said.

Whew! Dodged that bullet. Now he certainly had my attention.

"Where's he going to be?" I jumped in.

"Well he's staying at the Hilton, and first thing in the morning he's going to jog to Coffee Call and stop in to get beignets and coffee," he answered.

Coffee Call was, and is, a local favorite morning or night stop in Baton Rouge on College Drive near the center of the city. The hotel Clinton was staying at, now a Marriott, is on a side street about a half mile away.

As soon as that call ended, I was on the phone with the ever patient Ken "Kenny" Brumfield, the weekend photographer I worked with, who was basically teaching me how to be a TV reporter as I was doing the job. (Thank God for Kenny!)

Kenny was psyched. We would meet at Coffee Call early in the morning and walk over to the street Governor Clinton would be jogging along. Then we'd figure out how to get our one-on-one with him, with the other local reporters none the wiser.

I remember putting on my best purple power suit with matching 4-inch heels that morning. I meant business, even as I had no idea yet how the business worked. Right or wrong, the heels always made me feel taller on the inside. Whatever works.

Sure enough, here came Bill Clinton, taking his signature campaign morning jog, this time wearing an LSU t-shirt and surrounded by LSU students jogging too, with an entourage of national press photographers in tow.

Former President Bill Clinton jogs with LSU students in Baton Rouge while on the campaign trail for the Democratic nomination in 1992. (Courtesy: WAFB-TV)

Plan A in getting him one-on-one didn't pan out so well. I told Kenny to start rolling, then I jutted out into the street holding my microphone, and started jogging alongside the governor. Yes, in my 4-inch heels. Yes, with the network photographers looking on, cringing in horror and disbelief.

Understand also that the microphone cord was attached to the camera Kenny was holding, so he had to keep pace with the governor and me while trying to point and shoot a huge camera. I can't say for sure, but I have to believe Kenny was cursing me under his breath, asking himself why he got stuck with the rookie.

So picture Governor Clinton and I are jogging side by side, breathing heavily, as I blurt out what I can while dangling the microphone in front of him. I probably asked something like, "How are you feeling this morning, Governor?" Then probably something else equally as lame. As I recall Clinton tried to be kind and answer as he huffed and puffed, but it became quickly apparent that this was the wrong time and the wrong circumstance to get what I came for.

I darted back over to the side, with Kenny straggling behind me like a frustrated dog being pulled on a leash. I apologized to Kenny, he smiled with all the grace he could muster, and the two of us brainstormed a new idea.

Former President Bill Clinton sits with veterans inside Coffee Call in Baton Rouge during campaign stop in 1992. (Courtesy: WAFB-TV)

Plan B picked up as Governor Clinton arrived at Coffee Call. The place was fairly busy, and certainly packed as the governor entered, followed by all those photographers. Kenny and I were somewhere in the crowd behind the governor, when Kenny noticed a table of men wearing military hats sitting in the back corner of the restaurant. He suggested we set up on the other side of these veterans, thinking we'll get a much better camera angle if the governor walks toward us.

"If Bill Clinton doesn't walk up to that table full of veterans," Kenny said, "He doesn't deserve to be president."

As predicted, Governor Clinton walked right up to the table of a half dozen or so men. Here's where things got awkward, again.

I pulled out my microphone and pointed it at the governor, who was now sitting at the table. Then a short slim guy tapped me on the shoulder a little unnerved and said, "What are you doing?"

It was George Stephanopoulos. Yes, that George Stephanopoulos of ABC News. Back then, he was one of Governor Clinton's campaign advisors. Standing next to him was Clinton's campaign strategist James Carville, a Louisiana boy known as "the Ragin'Cajun," who also drew fame from that campaign.

George and James quickly admonished me. "This is a video op only," they said.

What's a video op? I thought. Again, don't judge if you're in the TV news business. I was very green at the time.

Kenny later explained to me that a video op is an opportunity for the media to get video, with the understanding no questions can be asked.

I guess James Carville saw my bewilderment, noted my age, and had a soft side for the local girl, a fellow Louisianan. He pulled me aside.

"I tell you what," Carville told me, "In a minute, Governor Clinton is going to walk over to the counter to fill his coffee cup, then walk out through that side door to the patio to talk to those students sitting out there. If you want to set up out there on the patio, I can't promise you he'll talk to you, but you can try to ask the governor a question."

Quick note: Interesting that the whole visit to this coffee house was very well choreographed in advance. The world of politics.

Kenny and I got into place on the patio by the students, and just as Carville said, Governor Clinton filled his coffee cup at the counter, then walked over to and through that side door, the crowd of press photographers still in lockstep behind.

"Governor," I said a little timidly, as he walked out onto the patio.

He walked right up to me, just as I'm pretty sure Carville suggested he do. The *why* didn't matter. It was "go time."

I fired off a question. He started answering.

Now it was chaos.

Former President Bill Clinton answers question outside Coffee Call in Baton Rouge as then campaign advisor George Stephanopoulos looks on during campaign stop in 1992. (Courtesy: WAFB-TV)

At this stage of the campaign, Governor Clinton was embroiled in the Gennifer Flowers controversy. She had accused the married politician of having an affair with her.

Photographers were jumping over tables and knocking over chairs, pulling out their microphones to get in place for this chance to ask a question.

As the governor finished answering my question, everyone was in place and started firing off their questions. The governor kept his eyes on me and started answering my second question.

The adrenalin was rushing through me. I was doing this!

As Clinton finished answering, the crowd of press photographers had to have drowned me out, as we all at once shouted out questions again.

Once again, the governor stayed focused on me, and yes, he took the local girl's THIRD question, ignoring the national press.

Again *why* he was focused on me didn't matter. I had to keep going.

Now here's where I take you into the mind of a budding reporter. I wasn't hearing a word the governor was saying at that point. The wheels in my head were turning a hundred miles an hour. All I could think about now was that I had to get a reverse cutaway.

The reverse cutaway is the shot of the reporter listening intently as the person she's interviewing speaks to her. In this case, the camera would be set up behind Clinton and shoot wide to show that he was speaking directly to me. It's proof of performance. It shows the reporter got the subject to answer HER question.

I elbowed Kenny. "Get the cutaway!"

This was apparently easier said than done. He had photographers on both sides of him, underneath him and on top of him. Bodies were blocking him in every direction. He started to elbow his way out of the web of legs and arms and cameras when… IT happened.

Kenny got pushed by one of the photographers into me, which pushed me into Bill Clinton, which caused Bill Clinton to spill his freshly poured cup of hot coffee all over himself.

"Ahh!" He yelled.

Picture a scene from "I Love Lucy." I'm Lucy, of course.

All at once I was nervously patting down the future president with my notepad, trying to wipe the coffee off of his shirt and pants as I repeated over and over again, "I'm so sorry. I'm so sorry."

This continued until Kenny was on the other side of Governor Clinton in place for the golden reverse cutaway shot. Then like a lightning flash, I quickly and abruptly stood tall, my apologetic grimace suddenly morphing into the serious newswoman I'm-listening-intently-to-your-every-word-as-I-nod face.

Reverse cutaway shot of Former President Bill Clinton answering Julie O'Neill question during campaign stop in Baton Rouge in 1992 (Courtesy: WAFB-TV)

Hey, there would be only a couple of seconds to get my reverse cutaway, so I had to look the part of the smart, serious, newswoman quickly. That's TV news.

I don't remember much after that. We did go to the scheduled press conference later, but I was the only local reporter who had a one-on-one interaction with Bill Clinton that night on the news, and it made the bosses happy.

———————◇———————

It's surreal to think about now. Any brush with fame is cool. For one moment in time, I had the full attention of the most powerful man in the world for eight years. More than that, though, the experience rolled into place a nice big cornerstone in the assimilation of my boldness, which would rise up to true confidence over time.

A win is a win, however awkward it comes, as you're coming up in business.

Whether you're just starting out or starting something new, this is a time you have to force yourself to forgive your bumbling gaffes and focus on the big picture, knowing you're going to get better.

A win is a win, however awkward it comes, as you're coming up in business.

Celebrate your successes.

What I lacked in knowledge and experience that crazy day in 1992, I made up for in young, hungry doggedness, and that was enough for a win.

It's a lesson I like to share with the young…over coffee.

CHAPTER 4

THE NERVE OF MERV

The Media Giant's Practical Joke

You better know whom you're dealing with, and sometimes they had better too.

With just over a year under my belt in the news biz at WAFB-TV in Baton Rouge, I found myself faced with interviewing one of TV's biggest names, as the new host of the station's morning show.

Before Oprah Winfrey or Jimmy Fallon, people were watching Merv Griffin, and the legendary Mervyn Edward Griffin, Jr. was touring the local TV circuit, promoting his new book.

If you're not familiar with the late great Merv Griffin, no shame. Even all those years ago (early '90s), my bosses assumed that I didn't know who Merv Griffin was. After all, *The Merv Griffin Show came on the air* in the '60s and was mostly in syndication in the '70s and '80s.[3] More recently he had become a behind-the-scenes guy, the creator of *Wheel of Fortune* and *Jeopardy.* He was also a casino magnate, among his business triumphs that had his wealth estimated at atleast a billion dollars at one point.[3] (I'll get to the casinos in a moment.)

The day before I was to interview Merv, my news director (still Nick), who was probably trying to make sure

I didn't embarrass him or the station, suggested I go up to the general manager's office to meet the visiting Merv and acquaint myself with him in advance of our interview.

So up I went. A little anxious. Definitely excited to meet the one and only Merv Griffin!

What I could not have anticipated was that Merv had quite a sense of humor and was a bit of a practical joker. He, his manager, and my general manager lay in wait for my knock on the door.

Knock knock.

As the door opened to the three men standing there, Merv's manager, standing a little in front of the other two men, looked at me and said, "Hi I'm Merv Griffin."

Without missing a beat, I looked this man in the eye, as I put my hand out to shake his, and said, "Hi I'm Linda Carter." Then I turned to Merv and said, "And you are?"

All three men burst into laughter. I'd foiled their nefarious plot to fool the young newby to the biz, and in that moment I had won Merv Griffin's respect and admiration.

Note how humor somehow leveled the playing field. It's a wonderful and also a powerful thing to make someone laugh. When we can share that tickle inside with someone, suddenly we're united in our humanness and at ease with ourselves and each other.

It's a wonderful and also a powerful thing to make someone laugh.

I don't remember the conversation that followed, just that we all joked and laughed and shared stories, and I had this icon of the TV business primed for an interview.

As Merv sat down the next day to be the interviewee on my little local morning show set, we hadn't talked about what I would ask. Of course I would bring up his new book, but I wanted to get a little something more from him.

Part of my development in approaching my career with boldness was making a point to differentiate myself. I specifically remember someone telling me early on that pretty, young, pageant girl reporters were a dime a dozen. People love to put people in a box. If you want to bust out of that box and be seen, you have to own your uniqueness and spotlight it.

I can tell you that asking the questions everyone expects you to ask is boring to me. And I don't know what's worse than boring. Nothing special sprouts from ordinary. I was intentional about seeing and doing things differently and taking risks to be REAL in interviews. I learned the importance of being REAL as I first started anchoring the news.

Describing me as a "diamond in the rough," my news director brought in a TV news consultant named Bill Taylor to polish me up. Bill took me through the "Talent Growth Model" developed by Audience, Research and Development (AR&D), explaining it as climbing steps of a pyramid. When I think about it now, these steps apply on some level to winning people over in any business.

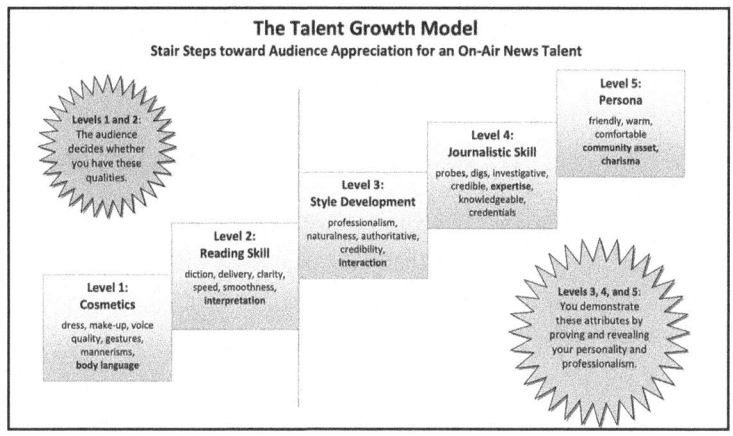

"Talent Growth Model" developed by Audience, Research and Development (AR&D), printed with permission of AR&D.

The first step is to make a good first impression in terms of the *Cosmetics*. People have to like– and not be distracted by– the way you look and sound in order to step up to the next level of the pyramid.

Next people judge whether they think you're good at what you do. For news anchors, they're paying attention to *Reading Skill*, and deciding whether they like the anchor's performance in terms of delivery and interpretation.

If you can get past those two levels of the pyramid, next people decide whether they like the way you come across. For news anchors, they're looking at your *Style Development*. Is this anchor professional, natural and credible?

The next step up the pyramid is where people decide whether they think you bring some expertise to your job. For an anchor they're looking at your *Journalistic Skill*. Does this anchor really dig in, investigate and have real knowledge about the subject matter? This is where people decide if they trust you, the golden tier for anyone in business, but there's still one more level to go.

The very top of the pyramid is that point at which people view you as a friend they feel comfortable inviting into their home. You're like family to them. For anchors this is *Persona*. It often takes years of showing you're involved in your community and care about the people in it. This is the peak. This is a relationship. This is where you get loyalty.

Building a relationship, a real connection with someone, is what gives you the edge over someone else who looks just as good as you, sounds just as good as you, and has just as good a product.

Building a relationship, a real connection with someone, is what gives you the edge over someone else who looks just as good as you, sounds just as good as you, and has just as good a product.

If you're a person who genuinely enjoys getting to know people, this comes naturally. It was natural for me, but I still had to overcome the temptation to be the very straight, stilted reporter-type when conducting interviews. There's a tricky balance between being professional and personal. I had to learn to keep a certain professional distance and still be real in conversation. This is not an easy task in the unnatural setting of TV interviews. You're sitting on a news set with cameras pointed at you. Someone is giving you time cues through an earpiece as you're talking and trying to listen to the person you're interviewing.

So how would I make my interview with Merv real and interesting?

I picked up from our conversation the day before that Merv had a very contentious relationship with Donald Trump. Back then, of course, the former president was known not for his politics, but for his resorts and casinos. He and Merv were fierce competitors in that business in Atlantic City. As the interview got going, I got Merv to talk about how and why that relationship became so adversarial, and saw the emotion building in him. I pushed his buttons a bit as a playful sister would at a family supper.

Note: I was creating a friendly, family atmosphere, like Merv and the viewers and I were all hanging out at home together, which is the top spot of the pyramid I told you about.

At some point Merv got really revved up and asked me, "Do you know what my long time fantasy has been?"

"What's that Merv?" I responded puckishly.

"In the dark of night, I want to climb up all the Trump casino signs and remove the T's," he answered with a mischievous school boy smile.

It took me a second to picture "rump!"

"Mr. Griffin!" I laughed.

Then he laughed.

What a moment!

When the interview ended, Merv shook his head smiling, looked me in the eye and said, "I'm going to tell you something, Julie. That was the best interview anyone's done with me."

I smiled back and made an immediate request. "Would you put that in writing, Mr. Griffin?"

"Sure will," he laughed, signaling for his assistant to grab one of his publicity photos from a briefcase.

And that's how I got the late great Merv Griffin to give me an autographed picture, stating, "Julie, You're the best!"

Signed picture of Merv Griffin given to Julie O'Neill

Merv Griffin, a man who had the cache to enter any room like he owned it, instead entered it like a family member, enabling me as a young nobody to do the same. Perhaps someone told *him* about the *pyramid*. Maybe it's just who he was. But I have to believe his talent for interacting with people in a familial way was a big part of what made him so successful. His sense of humor and comfort with himself propped him up to be the bold businessman he was.

I have always hung Merv's autographed picture at my desk at work as a relic of one of my wins. It's a reminder of the substantial dividends that taking the risk of doing things differently can pay.

It's important to pay attention to and track wins like these. Looking back now, I estimate that 9 out of 10 times I took a risk, it paid off. One out of 10 times it bombed and felt like hell. But 90 percent odds are really good odds and worth taking most of the time.

You have to develop the constitution to write off the failures and rejections, and just file them away. At some point I started a manilla folder into which I'd drop notes about those losses, so I could literally file them away. I still have the folder.

If you want to be bold in life, failures are important reminders to learn from, to file away, but not to see hanging on the wall. I've said previously that remembering and celebrating our successes is important to building boldness. I also recommend you pay attention to your percentages of wins to losses when you take a gamble. I bet it helps you win more often.

The ink from the picture Merv signed for me has faded over the decades, but this experience left an indelible mark on my spirit. I'll never forget his kindness and what he modeled for me.

Nor will I ever forget that at one moment in time I had the nerve to school Merv! You bet he learned whom he was dealing with.

CHAPTER 5

TIME TO THROW
A HAIL MARY

My Interview with a Saint

If I'm going to talk about the bold leaps it took to land the big interviews, this was the mother of all of them. How could I ever top a conversation with Mother Teresa?

Now Saint Teresa of Calcutta, all the world knows her as a holy woman who was dedicated to serving the poor, but after studying her life since my interview with her some thirty years ago, I believe I had a brush with the boldest, most influential businesswoman of our time.

It was the fall of 1992, my first year of full time work as an anchor/reporter for WAFB-TV in Baton Rouge. Several of us reporters, producers, and managers sat in the morning news meeting to brainstorm the coverage we'd bring following the death of the city's beloved bishop.

Bishop Ott was a kind and gentle man. He had reached out to people of all faiths, and was widely regarded as the true leader and unifier of the city. His cancer diagnosis a year before had been a heart-wrenching blow. All the public prayed and followed the progress of his treatments as we watched him approach the inevitable with hope, faith and grace. It was said that he taught us how to live and taught us how to die. Our coverage would require a half-hour special: *Bishop Stanley Joseph Ott: The Good Shepherd.*

So what would we include in these 30 minutes? What could we add that was unique and moving? Everyone we'd interviewed said Bishop Ott was the person they most admired. I suggested we include an interview with the person *he* most admired– Mother Teresa. She had visited Baton Rouge years before to set up a local chapter of her Missionaries of Charity. This was long before my entrance into the news business, but I had remembered the footage of the bishop looking as giddy as a school boy as he greeted this nun.

Bishop Stanley Joseph Ott welcomes Mother Teresa upon her visit to Baton Rouge in 1985. (Courtesy: WAFB-TV)

I made my case to my colleagues that it made perfect sense to reach out to Mother Teresa for an interview. Another reporter in the meeting chuckled with an eye roll and said, "I tell you what. You get Mother Teresa, and I'll get the pope."

I chuckle now when I think back to my reaction. If I was resting comfortably in my chair before, I was sitting up straight now, shoulders back. Something within the psyche suddenly rears forth like a stab through the shoulder blades when a competitive person is issued a challenge. Worse than anything I hate to be predictable, but like a Pavlovian dog my bell had been rung, and the pursuit was on to get Mother Teresa for the special.

My first call as it turns out was the only one I needed to make. It was to my friend Mark Blanchard at the Baton Rouge Diocese. We hadn't really known each other that long, but developed a good rapport as I covered the late bishop's cancer fight. Mark was one of those people who enjoyed connecting with people, and he seemed to know everybody in the diocese and everything that was going on.

"You're in luck," Mark told me.

He went on to say that a local photographer had just spent weeks doing a photo shoot with Mother Teresa and her nuns in Calcutta. Mark said he would reach out to this photographer on my behalf and see if he couldn't get me a good phone number. Within a few hours I had it, the home phone number for the Missionaries of Charity in Calcutta. I still have it in an old rolodex (remember those?). It's filed under "Moma T."

I decided, with the time difference, that I would need to wait until evening to make the big call, in order to catch the good sisters first thing in the morning halfway around the world. All day I thought about the possibility of speaking to Mother Teresa, praying that I would actually get to talk to her. This to me was something profound. She was touched by God so directly. I took it all in, as I thought through what I would ask her.

Hours later I sat on the news set, mic'd up and listening through my earpiece with great anticipation as the director in the booth dialed the long number.

Someone answered. "Hello."

"Hello! May I please speak to Mother Teresa?" I asked.

"This is Mother Teresa. Who is this?"

Whoa. Hit the brakes. Did she just answer the phone? Didn't expect that.

I had chills. I felt out of breath.

How do I start?

I knew the introduction I needed to make wasn't as simple as giving my name. It went something like...

"Hello Mother Teresa...I'm calling from the United States...in the state of Louisiana...I'm a news reporter...my name is Julie O'Neill."

The conversation went south quickly. Mother Teresa had suffered a recent stroke and was clearly still very much in the recovery process. She was confused. I kept trying to explain who I was and why I was calling. Nothing registered for her until I said, "Bishop Stanley Ott has died."

That did it.

"He was a very holy priest, and very faithful to the Holy Father," Mother Teresa said right back.

Thank God, I thought. She remembered him.

She said a little something I could use for the station's special, but that wasn't enough. As I worked to get more, Mother Teresa grew more and more frustrated. I knew I wouldn't be able to keep her on the phone much longer. Frankly I was feeling her anxiety myself. I wanted to let her off the phone out of compassion. Still I was so close and felt such pressure to get something I could use for the half-hour special that would honor this wonderful bishop's legacy.

I kept vigilant, as I tried to ease Mother Teresa's frustration.

HOW do I get this?! I was screaming inside.

Mother Teresa had started saying some words you say as you're about to hang up the phone, when it hit me.

I know how to put her in her comfort zone. This is Mother Teresa. Just ask her to pray!

"Mother Teresa, before I let you go," I said in a soft voice, "Would you please say a prayer for the people of Baton Rouge for healing and peace at the loss of Bishop Ott?"

The words poured out of her immediately.

A nice…long…beauuuuuutiful…prayer.

My effort to reach out to Mother Teresa added a solemn and fitting touch to my station's half hour special. That was the goal. But the experience of actually getting this international icon on the phone gave me so much more going forward as a professional. It set in me the mindset of being bold going forward. I now knew nothing nor no one was out of reach. I believed I could get the interview, and I got it. That's some pretty good positive reinforcement there.

Looking back, this encounter also bolstered my self-trust, another important building block of living boldly. While under great pressure to get a soundbite, the idea to ask Mother Teresa to pray seemed to come out of nowhere. It was instinctual. Somehow I knew how to make her comfortable, and that helped both of us. A win win.

Instincts are powerful speakers to be listened to. We now live in a Google world where we can look up anything online. We oughtn't lose sight of the great information we have stored up within ourselves.

We oughtn't lose sight of the great information we have stored up within ourselves.

As I've researched gut instinct, I've seen the scientific community giving it a lot more attention in recent years. An article in Harvard Business Review, *How to Stop Overthinking and Start Trusting Your Gut*, describes the "deep neurological basis for intuition." Author Melody Wilding writes, "Scientists call the stomach the 'second brain' for a reason. There's a vast neural network of 100 million neurons lining your entire digestive tract. That's more neurons than are found in the spinal cord, which points to the gut's incredible processing abilities." (Wilding, 2022)[4]

We can build self-trust more quickly by paying attention to just how often we have a positive result when we tap into our gut instincts.

Through the years my brush with a saint has brought many more gifts. I was asked years ago, following Mother Teresa's death, to voice the audiobook of her Novena, *Jesus is My All in All*. It inspired me to read books and articles about her life and what this woman who was described as "ordinary" early on in her life accomplished.[5]

What later made Mother Teresa extraordinary to all the world was her willingness to boldly pursue the vision God gave her for her life. It took her two years to get permission from the Catholic Church to start the Missionaries of Charity. She wrote letter after letter, insisting that she be allowed to start a religious congregation that didn't just serve the poor, but lived among them.[6]

At the time of Mother Teresa's death, her congregation had missions in 123 countries[7], including Iraq, where she was invited in 1991 to set up a home for mentally and physically handicapped children in a Baghdad mansion owned by the government under Saddam Hussein.[8] That's influence. We can certainly learn about love and sacrifice from this saint, but we can also learn about boldness.

————————◇————————

When my phone call ended with Mother Teresa, I raced to the newsroom to take my victory lap, screaming with jubilation.

"I just talked to MOTHER TERESA!" I yelled out.

Most cheered. One person in the newsroom barked back, "She's just a person."

(There's always one)

No you're just a person, I thought. I wasn't going to let anyone or anything steal a profound life moment from me.

The best part of my interview with Mother Teresa was how it ended. Feeling great relief after she finished her prayer, I thanked her for her time and told her what an honor it was for me to speak with her. Then she had the last words–

"God bless you."

I get that this is a common valediction for a religious person, but as far as I was concerned I had just been blessed by a saint. And I truly was.

CHAPTER 6

GIVE THAT GIRL
A GOLD CARD

Time to Take Charge

You gotta love a time of your life when everything you touch turns to gold. I couldn't have scripted my start in TV news any better. But like any good story, the twists and turns were coming. The plot thickened as the time had arrived to renew my contract in Baton Rouge.

Oh the fun of contract negotiations! When I explain how these work to young people starting out, I like to use a ballroom dancing metaphor. It is very much a dance that will conclude with a graceful dip, an awkward pose, or one of you waltzing out the door. If you're not bold enough to at least make your partner think you can and will waltz out, you're dead on the dance floor.

I had some pretty sweet dancing shoes on at this point in my career. The morning show ratings at my station in Baton Rouge had tripled during my time on the set. I actually got a call from the news director at a competing station, looking to lure me over to anchor his morning show. I said no. I would be loyal to the guys who gave me my break. But money does talk, and it was actually a letter I received from a credit card company that helped me determine what kind of money I would ask for from my bosses moving forward.

I had applied for an American Express Gold Card, and received a letter of rejection. The reason given was that the applicant must earn a minimum of $30,000 a year. I was making $20,000.

Oh it was ON now. Rejected?! I was going to get that Gold Card.

The day came to sit across a table from Nick Simonette in his office once again. It had been two and a half years since he'd hired me and he couldn't have been happier with me. Nick started our negotiations with glowing remarks. I'd done well. And so on, and so on. For this reason he said he was going to offer me something he'd never offered an employee before. A whopping 10 percent raise.

Ok, I'm not one to ever boast about having a good math brain, but it's not that difficult to come up with ten percent of 20k.

Just $2000 a year more?
Seriously?

The opening offer was disappointing and far short of my goal, but I understood that Nick's role was to keep my salary as low as possible. It was up to me to demand as much as he was willing to pay.

It was just the start of the dance and I wanted to keep it graceful. I grew up in the South where you're taught that you get more bees with honey than vinegar. I've always understood that being bold doesn't require you to be brash. It's best if the person deciding your income has the genuine desire to work

Being bold doesn't require you to be brash. It's best if the person deciding your income has the genuine desire to work with you and keep you happy.

with you and keep you happy. In this case I wanted Nick to *want* our waltz to end with a dip, and not me waltzing out the door.

"Well thank you, Nick. I appreciate that offer, but here's the thing…"

I went on to build my case, channeling that teenage girl inside who could always talk Dad into slipping her a 20 dollar bill before going out with friends for the night. We were a middle class working family, but Daddy's desire to be my hero always overshadowed his bankroll. I hoped my boss would want to be my hero too.

It's interesting to me now how the dynamic changed between me and my bosses over the years. As I got older and more experienced I related to my male and female bosses more as equals, though of course with due respect. In my early years, though, I engaged with older managers more like a child would with a parent. Right or wrong, Nick was a father figure to me and so that's how I approached him. It didn't necessarily weaken me in negotiations though.

In a humble, gentle tone I talked to Nick about the increase in the morning show ratings during my time as host. I talked about the long hours I'd worked, always with enthusiasm, to get great content into the other newscasts. I talked about the ideas I had to build on the successes I'd had. Then I spoke from the heart. I told him about the Gold Card.

"I want to share something that happened to me a week ago, Nick."

I took him through the Gold Card rejection letter story. How a person with my drive and dedication deserves Gold. Blah blah blah, I went on…

"I need to make 30-thousand dollars to get the Gold Card…"

"I'm worth this, Nick…"

"Let me show you how happy you're going to be in a year that you invested in me…"

He listened and nodded with some approval as he gave me the same paternal look of pride he'd given me when he first hired me. The conversation ended quickly, though. He'd have to take a number as high as 30k upstairs to the general manager.

The next meeting came a few days later.

Up the stairs I trotted, a 24 year old young woman now having to negotiate with both of my significantly older male bosses, the news director and general manager (GM). I'll admit it. I was nervous to the point of shaking a bit during this round of talks.

The two men sat on one side of the big desk in the GM's office. I sat on the other side and resigned myself to stay quiet and listen. They offered a 3-year deal. 23k the first year. 25k the second. 27k the third.

I tried to stay stone-faced as I heard the numbers, but they had to see the disappointment in my eyes.

The GM took the lead from there. He made it very clear he loved me and valued me, just as the news director did. "But," he explained, "We just can't justify 30-thousand dollars a year for the morning anchor position."

This offer was aligned with what the budget is for a newscast, not what my value was in general, they explained. They said they hoped I would consider their offer carefully and decide to stay. I believed them and said I appreciated that they went as high as they could go. I told them I'd think about their offer and let them know. They sent me on my way with words very familiar in contract negotiations in my business and others.

"Consider this carefully, Julie," they said. " It's easier to find a job when you have a job."

What should I do?

I loved working in Baton Rouge, where all my family and friends were. *Maybe if I stick around long enough I'll move up to the position of evening anchor and eventually make better money*, I thought, as I rationalized taking less than I felt I deserved.

On the other hand, if I was going to be bold enough to leave a job before I had a job, this was the time of my life to do it. I was a single woman with no mortgage to pay and no kids depending on me for support.

Before making a really bold move, I knew I needed input from someone who was smart, whom I trusted, and who really knew me. I went to see Momma.

My mother has never been one to hold back an opinion, but she also hasn't been one to weigh in on everything I do and say. She certainly wasn't a helicopter parent as I grew up. She didn't check to see if I'd done my homework. She didn't give me a curfew. Heck, she didn't even wait up on weekends to make sure I got home at a reasonable hour. Her head hit the pillow at 10 o'clock each night and she slept soundly, trusting my good judgment as all manner of shenanigans might have been going on. She often said to me, and still does, "You have a good brain, Julie Catherine."

Not this day, though. As I told my mother about the station's final offer, she went into full-on Jo E. Mode. (Her name is Jo Elizabeth, so people call her Jo E.) Full-on Jo E. Mode means she had that look on her face that, back in the day, inspired my childhood friends to enter my house through my bedroom window. Jo E. can be very intimidating, even when she doesn't mean to be.

Momma didn't mince words. "Under no circumstances will you take that offer," she said to me, looking me straight in the eye. "If you don't believe in yourself now, you never will."

Well that was that. I wouldn't take the offer. I'd have to be bold, whether I wanted to or not this time. Because Momma said so. And as it turned out, my mother knew best. (Once again.)

Soon thereafter I got a call from a big time New York agent.

"Is this Julie O'Neill, the rockstar?"

This is how my first and only agent started as I answered the phone. I laughed out loud.

"Ha! Why yes it is," I responded. "And who might you be?"

The incomparable Peter Goldberg introduced himself. Then got direct and to the point as any agent worth his salt does.

"I've gotten two phone calls about you within the last week," he said.

Turns out the news director who'd tried to lure me to the competing station had called Peter to tell him to get me out of the market. Smooth move. He was going to get his morning show ratings back up one way or another. The other call Peter got came from a news director in New Orleans named Joe Duke, whom I'd recently been to see. Joe's station was under a hiring freeze, so he couldn't get me an hour east from Baton Rouge to The Big Easy, but he admired my work, and loved my grandmother. This was MawMaw Ragusa, on my mother's side. He'd been to MawMaw's house with the guys for hot southern biscuits after an LSU game years before. Small world. Joe didn't have an agenda. He just wanted to help me.

I signed with Peter and within a couple of weeks he had multiple news stations interested. The first that wanted to fly me in for an interview was a station in Miami. Peter called this "an interesting" option for me. WSVN 7News was the #1 Fox station in the country. It was known as the "flash and trash" station, where "if it bleeds it leads." This didn't sound like me, but I made the trip for the interview.

WSVN's studio was a sight to behold. Joel Cheatwood had taken charge. He was an up and coming heavyweight in broadcast news, criticized by some for his leaning toward the sensational side of news, but his style boosted ratings. You had to give him that. Each newscast showed the whole 7News staff scurrying around the 2-story newsplex, walking and talking, getting any and all breaking news on the air like lightning, no matter what story they were in the middle of. This was intimidating to small town Julie O'Neill.

WSVN's news director gave me a tour of the station. Then came a writing test, and he had me do a walk-and-talk report across the newsplex. I felt like I got through it all ok, but didn't feel like I nailed it. The news director was kind of a quiet guy. He was hard to read. I never got that moment where I felt like we struck a rapport. I returned to Baton Rouge dreading the inevitable conversation with my new agent that it didn't go so well. I would never have predicted the call I got from Peter a few days later.

"They loved you!" Peter said enthusiastically. "Joel Cheatwood wants YOU."

So much for my self awareness.

I shared my misgivings about the station with Peter and he understood them, but assured me Joel had a vision for a new segment focusing on kids that would not be sensationalized. Joel liked the warm and easy interaction I had with kids, as shown on the resume tape Peter had put together. (These days it's all digital, but back then the higher ups had desks stacked with resume tapes.) WSVN's news director was super happy with my audition, and he and Joel thought I'd be the perfect ChildWatch reporter. Well now, that sounded like me. I still had a gnawing feeling in my gut, but my contract in Baton Rouge was up and this would be quite the step up. No bold move comes without a little fear. It was *goodbye Baton Rouge, Miami here I come!*

Julie O'Neill's last broadcast on WAFB-TV's Daybreak with Kara Finnstrom, Jay Gormley, and Diane Deaton (left to right). (Courtesy: WAFB-TV)

I remember saying goodbye to my mother, assuring her I wouldn't give up on getting a job back in Baton Rouge someday. She said, "You'll never come home," revealing a little sadness. Then she quickly gathered herself and sent me off with the words she'd given before any of my bold adventures. "Go show 'em how the big girls do it."

Oh, and yes, I got my Gold Card.

CHAPTER 7

WELCOME TO
THE BIG SHOW

How do you like me now?

WSVN 7News had all the bells and whistles and excitement of a Vegas casino. Working here, I had a seat at the table with the real risk takers now. They were all doubling down. Everybody knew how to be bold.

*Julie O'Neill poses with some of the WSVN
gang in the newsplex in 1995.*

Miami is not "sin city," but I did get my first dose of mean girl treatment while there. One of the anchorwomen was downright nasty to me, because I had a similar haircut. I remember once she walked up to me and yelled, "Get out of my chair!" There was no "Would you please..." about it. Most of the anchors and reporters were good to me though, and embraced me as I joined them in the newsplex. You may recognize the names Rick Sanchez and Robin Meade. Both went on to the networks after their stint in Miami. Both were kind and friendly. Shepard Smith, later of Fox News fame, was the star reporter at 7News while I was there. Everybody loved and worshiped Shep. What he could do on the fly! Boy was he fun to watch! And he was such a generous human being, always willing to offer advice or encouragement. Although he did bash

Julie O'Neill shooting pool with then WSVN reporter Shepard Smith in 1995.

my LSU Tigers once in a while, as a Florida Gator guy. (If I cross paths with him again, my first words will be, "Hi Shep! Joe. Burrow.")

My ChildWatch segment took a while to get up and running. The bosses wanted community input and we did lots of brainstorming about what this segment would be and do. I loved helping to create it, and once launched, I couldn't believe the resources now at my disposal. I had two producers assigned just to my segment, to do all the set-up work. Meg Porter took the lead and Kris Lloyd assisted, both good friends and strong writers. They even wanted to write everything for me. "All you have to do is front this stuff," they told me. That I didn't go for. Writing was personal for me.

The ChildWatch team turned out some first class work, from kids' safety and health issues to solving truancy problems. Fast moving, hard-hitting stuff, almost always edited with music tracks underneath. Everything was going great with the segment, until one day it wasn't.

Ever had this happen at a job?

The news director who hired me got fired. The new news director had her own thoughts about the ChildWatch segment and didn't seem to think much of me. Funny how life is: one person thinks you're a hero and another thinks you're a zero. One special assignment she gave me probably didn't help matters.

Ok this was during the days of the O.J. Simpson murder trial in 1995. For my younger readers, O.J. had been a star NFL running back, broadcaster and actor, very popular with the public. He was now accused of murdering his former wife, Nicole Brown Simpson, and her friend Ron Goldman. 7News was dedicating wall to wall coverage. O.J. all day.

At this time Miami was also getting ready to host the Super Bowl, which would air on FOX. Some players would be coming to the 7News studio to tape promos, including then Kansas City Chiefs Running Back Marcus Allen. Allen had just made headlines in the O.J. trial. He was friends with O.J. and O.J.'s former wife, Nicole, and had even gotten married at O.J.'s Rockingham estate.[9] Just before Marcus Allen was to visit the 7News studio, Faye Resnick released her book, *Nicole Brown Simpson: The Private Diary of a Life Interrupted*, in which she wrote that Allen had an affair with Nicole.[10]

The day before Marcus Allen was to shoot promos at WSVN, the new news director called me into her office. She told me she had something special for me to do the next day that had nothing to do with my ChildWatch segment. As I recall, all I was told at that time was that I should come to work the next day dressed to kill.

As I arrived to work the following day, looking my best and ready for action, I learned of my assignment. It was explained to me that Marcus Allen and some other pro football players were coming to shoot promos, but there were rules in place that prohibited WSVN from asking them any questions while on the station property. My job would be to follow Marcus Allen off the property and find an opportunity to ask him a question on camera. The question was, "Did you have sex with Nicole Brown Simpson?"

Wow! Ok, I was taken aback, as you probably are right now. It took me a moment to process this assignment.

"If anybody can get him, you can Julie," I heard from the boss.

That part felt good. The assignment sure didn't. *I'm going to ask a man if he had sex with the victim of a brutal murder?* I thought. *What has my broadcast journalism career come to?*

I sat in a vehicle in the station's parking lot with a photographer who was equally if not more disgusted by our assignment for the day. That would make this whole thing even more difficult to stomach, let alone pull off. We were pretty quiet, both probably going over all of this in our heads, as we lay in wait for Marcus Allen to leave.

When the time came, we pulled out of the parking lot and we were on the move, following Marcus Allen through the streets and highways of Miami. It was about 25 minutes into the drive, when the car Marcus Allen was riding in pulled into the parking lot of a restaurant/bar. He went in. We went in. As it turned out there were other media there for some kind of event my station apparently didn't know about or wasn't invited to. We would fit right in with our camera, but no one was rolling video or asking questions. I felt swallowed up in discomfort, as I thought of the idea of suddenly putting a camera in Allen's face in front of everyone and asking, "Did you have sex with Nicole Brown Simpson?"

My photographer and I decided it was just not the time and place to do what we were sent to do. We would hang out a while, keep an eye on Allen, and maybe catch him in the parking lot as he left.

In the meantime, I mingled with the crowd of mostly NFL players and their people to loosen up a bit and try to enjoy the moment. Feel things out. I approached Marcus Allen, who was standing with a small group of men I didn't recognize, and we had a short exchange. He was likable as we shared a little small talk. I don't remember what was said, just that as I looked into his bright, friendly eyes I thought, *poor guy doesn't know he's talking to the devil.* The conversation certainly didn't help me muster the nerve to do what I'd come to do.

I walked over and found a seat at the bar. Before long, Dolphin quarterback Dan Marino was sitting next to me. The two of us chatted it up for a few minutes, a fun distraction until he was called away. Then I was alone with myself again. As the clock ticked, the gnawing in my stomach grew worse, not better.

My news director was right. *I could do this. But should I?* I kept asking myself, until the bold decision came. I pulled aside the man who seemed to be Marcus Allen's handler. I told him that he *might* want to slip out a back door with Allen, because a reporter *might* be waiting in the parking lot with a cameraman to ask Allen a question that *might* make him uncomfortable. And that was that.

Allen slipped out the back. The photographer and I returned to our station, as failures. No hero status for Julie.

I call my decision a bold one, because it was tough to go back to my boss empty handed. I'm very competitive and have a high need to please. My news director had entrusted this assignment to me and I didn't just fail, I failed on purpose. I shot myself in the foot.

What trumped everything at the end of the day, was that I had to survive more than I had to succeed. We all have a line we cannot cross. Sometimes we don't know what that line is until we get right up to it. We're flawed as human beings, and so we sometimes give into the temptation to compromise ourselves to a certain extent, but doing what I was asked to do felt like a complete about-face from my values.

Maybe you've been in this situation or will be someday in your job. What's really the bold move? The clearer you are about who you are and what you believe, the clearer that answer will be for you. I think in the bigger picture of life's happiness and contentment, there's just no survival if you sell your soul.

I think in the bigger picture of life's happiness and contentment, there's just no survival if you sell your soul.

I still feel I did the right thing, but as is so often the case in life, that sometimes has consequences of its own. Things got progressively worse for me in Miami. The mojo was gone between me and the top managers. I felt their disapproval daily, like they didn't want me there. I didn't fit in. And I was overwhelmed by it.

I called my agent, Peter, and asked him to get me out of there. He called my news director and she agreed to let me out of my contract. I felt broken.

As it happened, that feeling of worthlessness wouldn't last long though.

Within a few days, I got a call from Peter, my agent, as I sat despondently at my little desk in the upper deck of the newsplex. This call would make things feel a lot better quickly. "WABC in New York wants to meet you," he couldn't wait to tell me. The mothership had landed.

"Holy shit!" I'm sure I screamed. I couldn't wait for that interview. Cue the music: "Start spreadin' the news..." I personally like the Liza Minnelli rendition of that song the best. And yes, I have her "New York, New York" album. And yes I played it and danced around my apartment in the days before that interview. And yes, on the day of the interview, I sang "New York, New York" as I walked up Manhattan's Upper West Side in my long black wool coat and big dark sunglasses, pretending I was a star. It's all true.

What a fantastic day it was!

I got to tour the #1 ABC O&O (owned and operated) station in the country. I met with every manager. My tour of the WABC studios even included the set of *Live with Regis and Kathie Lee* (the originals of the show *Kelly and Ryan* would later host) and I even got to sit on Kathie Lee's stool. SO fun!

As the day was coming to an end, I had a sit-down interview with WABC's news director. At one point his face turned serious, and he asked me why my news director in Miami was willing to let me out of my contract. I hadn't anticipated that question. Here was a sudden opportunity to take a bold leap of faith.

I took a deep breath and just said it. "I'll be honest with you. She's not a fan of mine."

I took another breath in anticipation of what would certainly not be a positive reaction from this man holding my life in his hands. I was already thinking about what I could say to mitigate the damage. His response stunned me.

"Well I'll be honest with *you*," he said. "I'm not a fan of *hers*."

Whew! What were the chances? I couldn't believe it. Being dead honest with this man was like hitting on a 16 in blackjack when the dealer is showing a face card. It's the right thing to do in terms of your odds, but it never feels good. Instead of busting, I hit 21! We had a great conversation after that.

Now there was just one more interview to get through, this one with WABC's general manager, the top guy. He made a concerted effort to get me comfortable immediately, not holding back on how much he admired my work. It was all good. As I left his office, though, he made a point to tell me how much he wanted me to stay in touch with him.

"You call me anytime you have any questions," he said. Those didn't sound like the words of someone getting ready to hire me.

A few days later back in Miami, the call came from my agent, Peter, that I did not get the job. The position that was open was for WABC's morning show. They were hiring a reporter who would be live on location each day. I didn't have live shots on my resume tape because I didn't do live shots for the ChildWatch segment. Peter said WABC wanted me to go to a station where I could do live shots every day, and talk to them again in a year.

The station I would go to next offered the perfect opportunity. I actually turned down an anchor job in a different market, to be the nightside reporter for WCPO in Cincinnati, where I could do live shots on top stories every night at 11:00. This would look like a step backward from a much larger market such as Miami, but I believed the opportunity in Cincinnati was a step forward to my goal of working in New York.

I always tell young people, your decision about where to go next in your career should be based on where you want to be after that. Perceptions and paychecks are secondary to strategizing toward the big prize.

Perceptions and paychecks are secondary to strategizing toward the big prize.

In Cincinnati, I'd be working for Jim Zarchin, the news director, and Stuart Zanger, the assistant news director. Both had worked in New York and knew how to prepare me for it. They needed a replacement for a reporter who'd just left the station for Cleveland. Gretchen Carlson. Yep, that Gretchen Carlson, who would end up at FOX News and go on to start the #MeToo movement. Gretchen had been Miss America, and I think Jim Zarchin liked the idea of bringing in a similarly competitive young woman who had a strong background of performing. He especially liked that I'd previously lived in Cincinnati, while I was studying musical theater at U.C.'s College Conservatory of Music.

Team Zarchin and Zanger promised to critique my scripts and make me a first class writer. This felt right. In time, I'd learn these two men were true to their word and great to work for and learn from.

Reunion party in 2022 for WCPO employees of the 1990s. (From left to right: Stuart Zanger, Dennis Janson, Julie O'Neill and Jim Zarchin)

I had seven'd out at 7News, but a bold new adventure awaited.

I remember going to visit my Gamma O'Neill just before starting the new job. She was in her late eighties and had dementia at this stage of her life, but she became lucid for a moment and knew who I was. She took my shoulders into her hands, looked into my eyes, and said, "Your husband is in Cincinnati." Then the former opera singer launched into "Climb Every Mountain" from *The Sound of Music*. I stood there in shock and awe as she sang the whole thing, nailing the "Mother Superior" high note at the end! Maybe it's corny and melodramatic for others, but it was a life moment for me. And she was right. I'd never make it to New York. I'd meet my husband, settle down, and raise my children in Cincinnati, "The Queen City."

CHAPTER 8

HOME ALONE WITH A KILLER

Canvassing a Neighborhood Could Prove Fatal

It was a dynamic scene. Cops crawling everywhere. There had been a murder.

Several years now on the job in Cincinnati, I felt fully alive reporting, especially when arriving at an active crime scene. All senses heightened. Competitive juices surging. Confident self-talk blaring. I would be the reporter at the scene who'd get what no one else could if it killed me. It certainly could have this particular sunny day in November of 1997.

Shanon Marks was a beautiful, sweet, smart 29-year-old woman, living with her new husband Norman in their first home in Cincinnati's East Walnut Hills neighborhood. All the homes were different here, like all the people inside them. I remember reading that's why they picked it. Theirs was a small, quaint Victorian style home, which from the curb imbued warmth, love and friendship. One Wednesday morning, Norman kissed his wife goodbye and left for work as she was still getting herself ready to leave for her job as an analyst for Cincinnati based Procter and Gamble. When

Norman returned to the home later that day, he walked into images not comprehensible to the soul. Shanon had been brutally beaten to death with a baseball bat in their bathroom.

I remember all too well the day I was assigned to cover the story a few days into the investigation. It was a huge story with tremendous public interest, and the Cincinnati Police homicide detectives were being very tight-lipped.

My partner for the day was the legendary Charles "Chic" Poppe, a Peabody Award winner. He slept with three emergency scanners in his bedroom and had one in his car. He was ready to spring into action at any time day or night when news happened, sometimes arriving at scenes before the police did. Chic and I worked well together, both Type A personalities. Determined to get something substantial for the 6 o'clock news that night, Chic and I agreed that he would keep his

Peabody Award winning photographer Charles "Chic" Poppe

camera pointed at the house to capture anything the detectives brought in or out. I would canvas the neighborhood, knocking on doors to see what if anything I could find out about Shanon and the investigation.

I had just started down the sidewalk when I saw an older woman leaving her home right around the corner from the Marks house.

"Excuse me, Ma'am…I hope I'm not intruding…"

I went into my introduction and why I was there. The woman was kind and sympathetic, deeply pained by the horrific crime that had happened so close by. She told me her grandson had heard their dog barking around the time of the murder. She said he was in the house and it was ok to go in and talk to him. She got in her car and left. I went in.

"Hello!" I announced myself as I spotted the young man in the kitchen. "Your grandmother said I could come in." I told him who I was and why I was there and he invited me to sit down at the kitchen table.

"What's your name?" I asked.

"Rayshawn Johnson," he answered.

I got the spelling down on my notepad and we talked for around ten minutes I suppose. He seemed shy and a bit uneasy, so I needed to get him comfortable with me before asking him to give me an on-camera interview.

At some point I relayed to him what his grandmother had told me, and in somewhat broken, nervous speech he confirmed that he did hear the dog around the time Shanon Marks was killed. When I got around to asking him to talk to me about that on camera, I was surprised that he seemed perfectly willing.

Rayshawn and I left his grandmother's house, found Chic on the sidewalk outside the Marks house, and did the interview. *Success*, I thought. I had something substantial for the 6 o'clock news and I didn't have to bother the detectives or the victim's family to get it.

It was a couple of days later I was knocked to my knees in the most chilling moment of my career.

Watching my station's 11 p.m. news, reporter Lynn Giroud came on with breaking information on the Marks case. She said detectives had made an arrest.

I was glued to the set.

Suddenly there was video on the screen of my interview with Rayshawn.

Then came Lynn's next words.

"Ironically the suspected murderer gave our Julie O'Neill an interview a couple of days ago."

My knees buckled. I heard myself let out a blood curdling scream. My whole body shook. I struggled to catch a breath. I had been alone in a house with the murderer and nobody knew where I was at the time.

The moment I heard Lynn Giroud utter those words, while looking at the video of me with Rayshawn on the TV screen, I got smacked with the reality that I could've been killed too.

I'd already felt a connection to Shanon. We were roughly the same age, both professional women. The more I learned of the details of what happened to her, the sicker I felt. I guess when we see ourselves in the victim, the story feels more personal. Now I'd been face to face with the man who did this to that poor woman.

It later came out in one report that Rayshawn revealed in his confession he had seen Shanon jogging in the neighborhood in the days before the murder, and had been watching her. According to that report, he said that on that fateful Wednesday morning "a voice" told him to kill her, so he entered an unlocked door of the Marks home and did just that.

Crazy!

"A voice" told him to do it?!

So random!

Shanon had no chance. She was at the start of a beautiful life with a new husband and home and a great job she'd worked hard to get. *She's gone because a voice told somebody to kill her? Why didn't a voice tell him to kill me?* I thought. There was a guilt and a fear now, to go along with the grief I felt for a woman I never even knew. (Note: The report of Rayshawn claiming "a voice" told him to commit the murder was later unsubstantiated. In subsequent reports by Cincinnati news outlets and court filings, it was revealed that Rayshawn confessed to killing Shanon and stealing money from her purse, because he needed money for drugs.[11]

It's a story that as a reporter and a person I could never let go. Many years after Shanon's murder, I reached out to Norman Marks to see if he would meet with me for lunch and talk. I can't just glaze over that, because mustering the courage to call him was a whole thing unto itself. Some things take more boldness than others and don't feel good in any way. If you think about it, difficult conversations may be the hardest things we approach in life. *What would I say when he answered? Should I really do this, knowing it will surface something so very painful for him?*

I had heard Norman's excruciating pain on the 9-1-1 call he made upon discovering Shanon's murder all those years ago. The raw, guttural agony in his voice was debilitating to listen to. I wanted to throw up. I can never unhear it. It's one reason there's debate in the media about whether or not to play certain 9-1-1 calls over the air, and if so, how much of the call should be aired. Not only do some of these calls potentially scar the listener, but it sometimes seems too big an invasion of privacy. Many argue you're crossing a personal boundary when you broadcast to the world someone's most vulnerable, helpless moment.

The reason I now wanted to have a conversation with Norman is that I felt very strongly that I needed to tell the story of what homicide detectives go through, living and breathing crime scenes like Shanon's on a regular basis. If that one 9-1-1 call haunted me, what must they go through? Part of their sacrifice to society is that they must see the horrific images from which the rest of us are sheltered. As a reporter, I saw a few very troubling images over the years that still have perfect clarity in my mind's eye. These detectives have catalogs of these images in their heads, which they must carry around their whole lives. On the days I covered the Marks murder I noticed a particular heaviness in the eyes of a couple of the detectives, like it could've been their daughter. The Marks case also felt like the right one to build the story around because of its randomness and how high profile it was.

The first thing I had to do was see whether the detectives were willing to open up about their emotional experience and how they cope. When I reached out to one of the detectives and explained what I wanted to do, he said he would be willing to do an interview on camera, IF the other detectives agreed to as well, and IF Norman Marks gave this his blessing.

I had to call Norman.

When Norman and I finally spoke by phone, I was surprised by how kind and strangely sympathetic *he* was to *me*, as he could apparently tell this call was a tough one for me to make. He said he remembered seeing me at the scene that November of '97. He said he appreciated how respectful I was, both to him and the detectives when they told me he did not want to talk to reporters. For that reason he said he would meet with me.

Those were moving and affirming words to hear. Sometimes quieting my competitiveness in favor of compassion and sensitivity meant losing key opportunities in my career. Now Norman was telling me that mattered to him, and even made a difference during the darkest time of his life.

The lunch I had with Norman that week was surreal. We met at the old Parker's Blue Ash Tavern in suburban Cincinnati, which sadly later closed down for good amid the pandemic. There was a good lunch crowd, plenty of robust chatter all around us. We were both dressed in business casual and fit in seamlessly with the lighthearted crowd, despite the weightiness of our meeting. I was nervous and very aware of his inner pain as we started to talk. It was healing for me to sit across from him in this normal setting being just a regular guy, having lunch, living his life. He was comfortable and settled. He had survived what happened, and though I knew what lurked inside him and always would, he seemed to have some hope and joy in his life all these years later. That was a great comfort to me.

Norman gave me his blessing to do the TV interview with the detectives on the case, and even said he would consider saying something on camera himself, because he wanted to express his appreciation for the way those detectives had treated him. But the TV interview never happened, because the lead detective later gave me a flat "no." I was right that this case was deeply important to him. It was his determined, pained eyes that I remembered most at the crime scene. He was not going to say anything to jeopardize any part of the case, because the death sentence was still being appealed. I respected that, and him. I had to let it go.

Though I didn't get the story, I'm glad I found the courage to reach out to Norman. It required a very different kind of boldness, because it risked pain for someone else. Some bold moves are not about psyching ourselves up, but about connecting deeply with our humility and humanity. As it turned out, Norman was comfortable meeting with me, and our lunch together gave me some peace about him. I'm forever grateful to him for sitting down with me and opening up, even if only just to me.

Some bold moves are not about psyching ourselves up, but about connecting deeply with our humility and humanity.

I started this chapter heralding my competitiveness as a reporter, out getting the story. I'll end it on a humble note.

Another reporter from a competing station had also done an interview with Rayshawn Johnson before the revelation that he was the murderer. It was Tricia Macke's interview that helped break the case. Detectives looked at the video of her story and noticed Rayshawn's shoes were the kind worn by the killer. He'd left a footprint at the scene. A little more investigative work had him locked up.

As it turned out, Tricia Macke got what no other reporter did at that crime scene. Not me. She was also smart enough to stay with her partner/photographer while canvassing the neighborhood. Lesson learned. However "exciting" a dynamic crime scene may feel, it's the scene of a tragedy to be approached with respect and caution. I could've learned that lesson the hard way. There's a difference between bold and stupid.

CHAPTER 9

ON THE FRONT LINES

This We'll Defend, Charlie

People ask me what my favorite interview of all was. Nope, not "Moma T." Not Merv. Not even Garth. (though my "friends in low places" know conversations with Garth Brooks over the years kept a smile on my face for weeks after!)

No, my favorite interviews were always with members of the military. Our valiant warriors. Something about the opportunity to sit down and go really deep with regular men and women who'd been to the darkest corners of the human experience. The courageous level of vulnerability many shared was something precious I always felt a greater responsibility to handle with care.

If I had to pick one, the best interview of all had to be with the late great Charlie Geraci, who was sitting beside his late wife Helen for our talk in 2014.

I learned of Charlie's phenomenal story of survival and hope in a conversation with their son Joe, whom I'd met years earlier. Joe had sold me jewelry from his shop in 1998. Nice man. We'd had friendly conversations from time to time. Then one day I got a call from him wondering if I might have interest in telling his father's story, as his dad was about to turn 90.

As Joe shared the story I listened in awe and utter disbelief. I mention this because in these minutes I felt a shrinking sense of disappointment in myself. I was learning that lesson once again that you never know how truly fascinating a person is until you make the intentional effort to get to know them. Success in life and work is all about taking time to develop real relationships with people. It's certainly true for a reporter. In any case, Joe was not just the jewelry guy anymore. I immediately set about getting the story he shared onto the air.

> *Success in life and work is all about taking time to develop real relationships with people.*

It was a cool, sunny October day. I arrived at the Geraci home with much anticipation. It was one of the many older homes on a tree-lined street that characterized the small city of Norwood, just north of Cincinnati proper. Norwood was a working man's industrial town in Charlie's day. He had made a living as a school teacher as his wife, Helen, ran the home.

Young Charles "Charlie" and Helen Geraci stand outside their Norwood home (Courtesy: Geraci family)

I received a warm welcome and sat down at the kitchen table with the married couple of 68 years. The table was covered with scrapbooks filled with photos I had previously asked them to get out for the interview. Old black and white pictures led across the table to color pictures, showing the evolution of photography in the love story of this couple from the Greatest Generation.

When I'd sit down with anyone, there would always be that period of maybe 15 to 20 minutes of just getting the person comfortable. No camera rolling. Just relating as people, noticing what's around and I guess sensing what I needed to do to assure this person felt safe to be truly authentic. It's hard to open up with a camera pointed at you. No one wants to look foolish. There's the pressure to say just the right thing. I'd almost always tell the person if they say anything they don't like, I won't use it. I meant that and it served me well in earning trust and delivering more meaningful stories.

As Charlie spoke, I watched Helen watch him and hang on his every word, nodding now and again as she sat quietly. I loved seeing the respect in her eyes. Charlie was a WWII hero. He'd been awarded three Purple Hearts and the Bronze Star. He served with Company D 9th Infantry, 2nd Indian Division. He was in the 2nd wave at Omaha Beach in Normandy. Helen had known Charlie since he was a boy before the war. His story started with the day he said he became a man.

Charlie was just 18 years old when he was baptized into the reality of war. Wading in the water up to Omaha Beach, he said the Navy was covering them, dropping shells, trying to keep them as safe as possible, but they were under heavy fire. He remembered wondering why these other men around him weren't getting up and getting out of the water. Then it hit him. They had been shot, and they were dead.

Charles "Charlie" Geraci (left) as a young soldier
during WWII (Courtesy: Geraci family)

Charlie's combat career wouldn't last too long afterward. Frankly put, he was blown up and sewn up three times in Northwestern France. He was finally put out of commission in Brest. His wounds were so severe, he'd been left in a ditch to die. He recounted how he cried out to his comrades, "I can live!" He pleaded with them to take him with them for care. There were so many wounded soldiers, hard decisions had to be made about who could survive and would be carried onward to get patched up.

Charlie's recovery would require years of hospitalization, enduring painful surgeries, bandaged up in body casts in between, with a question mark on whether he'd walk again. The greatest concern, though, was the more certain long-term prognosis from the doctors. They very plainly told him he should not expect to ever have children.

Now this is why I had to tell this story.

Within a couple of years, Charlie and his high school sweetheart, Helen, got married and went on to birth and raise

15 children in their Norwood home. Fifteen! And Charlie mentioned a couple of times, to make sure I noted, that all 15 were college graduates.

Charlie and Helen, as was true of so many of their generation, had run a tight ship. It was everyone at the table for family supper, a prayer before the meal, and NO getting out of line. "They all had a little different abilities," Charlie said, "…and their problems."

As Charlie continued on, his pleasant countenance suddenly morphed into the stern father's glare of younger years. "I had to go face to face with one or two of them to straighten them out," he said. Then he chuckled as he demonstrated the technique he had used now and again on a child at the dinner table. "I'd look down at them and give them 'the old evil eye' as they called it, and say, 'You're going to do what?!'"

The Geraci family gathers at the dinner table in
Norwood, Ohio home (Courtesy: Geraci family)

I looked over at the stern expression of approval on Helen's face. Then came a few words on the subject from the wife and mother's perspective. "He's an anchor, honey. Strong."

As long as people inhabit the Earth we'll debate what the best couple relationship looks like and the correct way to raise kids, but it's hard to argue against the Charlie and Helen united front approach.

———————◇———————

I was invited to the Mass of Celebration held in honor of Charlie's 90th birthday at Holy Trinity Church in Norwood a couple of weeks after our interview. It was packed, every pew filled with Charlie and Helen's kids, and their kids, and their kids. Their oldest son, Father Anthony Geraci, officiated the mass. What a birthday present it must have been for Charlie. So fitting for this man who lived boldly every step of the way.

The Geraci family poses for a picture on steps of Norwood, Ohio home in June, 2012 (Courtesy: Geraci family)

It's a profound thing as a reporter to be invited into someone's life experience. To be welcomed into parts of themselves they often haven't shared with their closest family and friends. That was the case with many war heroes I was honored to sit with over the decades. What I've learned most about the value of life I learned from them. And so I'll let Charlie have the last word in this chapter.

Charlie's secret to a life well lived, he told me, was the same thing that kept him alive on that battlefield in France 72 years prior. He kept looking forward to good things ahead. "Life is an experience," he told me. It's a happy experience if you look at it the right way."

CHAPTER 10

THE OVER AND UNDER ON SURVIVING

What are the Odds I'll Outlast This One?

There's an aura around any anchorwoman. A universal assumption it seems. She has the world by the tail. She leads the perfect charmed life. This is an illusion.

If I had a nickel for every time I got passed over for a promotion or sweat a contract renewal…

Ugh. I guess it's time to really get down into the weeds of the not so pretty part of this prized profession, and what helped me push through the angst in the office place.

I'll share one particular disastrous occasion I nostalgically refer to as "the double whammy." This one has all the drama.

It was 2016. I had been the weekend anchor for years. This actually had worked out well for me while I was raising children. I even got to anchor part-time for several years, which is unheard of in the business. But the kids were older now and the time had come to jump back into being a major player. Suddenly there were TWO openings for a weekday anchor position at the station.

All the planets were in alignment for me to take my career to the next level. The boss picked me to fill in for these positions and it was going exceedingly well. Ratings boosted. Viewer feedback was positive.

One of the openings was for the 4:00 p.m. newscast. I pitched an idea to the boss. I would co-anchor it with Tanya O'Rourke. Tanya was a bold one too. Very comfortable with herself. She had risen to main evening anchor status. Tanya and I had been competitors for promotions through the years. She always won. Whatever rivalry I might have felt earlier on had now morphed into a genuine admiration and friendship. WLW radio host Bill Cunningham had dubbed us

Anchors Julie O'Neill and Tanya O'Rourke at WCPO in Cincinnati in 2017

"the O girls." I'd tune into his show driving to or from work and hear him and longtime sports guy Seg "Segman" Dennison bantering on the radio, referring to us as "Tanya O-yeah O'Rourke" and "Julie O-yeah O'Neill."

Tanya and I would've knocked that show out of the park. It would've been smart, fun and unique, fronted by the two strong female faces of the station, I thought. Would've, could've, should've, but I struck out at the plate with that pitch. The bosses had a completely different vision for the show, and hired somebody from the outside to anchor it.

I was disappointed, but there was still that other weekday evening anchor position. Surely that one would be mine. I waited in anticipation for the good word. I felt strong and confident. The new news director knew talent. He'd been a talent scout for the company. He noticed my good work and seemed to be a fan of mine.

Then the day came. The new boss caught me for a quick conversation as I was walking to the studio to anchor the noon newscast. I was expecting to hear something about a scheduling issue or something about the content in the newscast I was about to do. I was utterly blindsided by what came out of his mouth. He told me he had hired someone else for the remaining open anchor position.

I stood there paralyzed. My mouth hung open.

There were a few conciliatory, complimentary statements about me mixed in as he continued to talk, but all I heard in that minute or two was that my career was over.

I struggled for words as my chest tightened. I asked why I didn't get the position. His answer would be something I could never forget. He said, "Because we have to win."

I think I physically buckled over. I know I paused in shock for a moment. Absolutely no words for that. *Did he just call me a loser?*

It was almost show time so there was no processing this. I had to hurry to the set to anchor a live newscast. What came next I'm not proud of.

I knew I had to put this out of my mind and deliver a professional show, but no self-talk could blare out, "Because we have to win."

With whatever grit I had, coupled with the grace of God, I somehow managed to get through the on-air part of the first block of the show. But as soon as the red light under the camera turned off for a commercial break, the earthquake hit, and there was no holding back the tsunami of emotion. The tears erupted. I had 2 to 3 minutes to cry out what couldn't be stopped, clean up my makeup, and perform for the next block of the show as we came back on-air.

This continued through commercial break after commercial break.

Longtime director Matt Luken was in the booth. The director is the person controlling every command and button push associated with getting a smooth show on the air. A lesser director would've been on the verge of a full-on panic attack at the edge of his seat, sweating out every second, as he was forced to constantly gauge whether he'd have to quickly add commercials or otherwise call for help to get another anchor to the set. Matt wasn't known for his soft edges, but during this newscast Matt was both cool, and kind. "Are you going to make it Julie?" he'd ask from time to time in a soft but reassuring voice piped through my earpiece. I'd nod my head and gain composure just in time for the red light to announce we were back on the air.

When the longest newscast of my career finally ended, no one watching from home knew a thing was wrong. Matt took care of me. He didn't speak of it to the managers. Now I just had to make it to an outer hallway, to the stairs, and down to the parking garage.

I remember sitting there in my minivan wondering whether I was ok to drive. I was so upset. When I finally made it home, the anger hit.

I don't have to tell you that anger is a dangerous thing. People are simply not their best selves while steeped in that emotion, and unfortunately it's the easiest emotion to get to in times of trauma. It's why, as a reporter, I remained quiet at many breaking news scenes when someone started yelling at me for being there. I understood that when people are in trauma, they need to get that emotion out. I arrived many times to good people's worst moments, and somehow knew to stay silent when their need to let it out was directed toward me. Sometimes in life you have to give a

Sometimes in life you have to give a person grace, stand still, and take the figurative punch to the stomach.

person grace, stand still, and take the figurative punch to the stomach.

Anyway, I was angry. *How dare my boss call me a loser.* (Not that those were his words, but it sure was my takeaway.)

Out came my laptop from my briefcase, and I started typing, the words pouring out. My news director was going to get one strong email.

Because we have to WIN kept spiraling in my head.

My email enumerated the big wins of my career. My news director might not see my talent and ability, but he was going to know about my wins, and he was going to get the details of them.

Within a few hours, I got an email response from the news director. He said we'd "have another conversation" about his decision to hire from the outside.

I responded with another email, stating that our next conversation would have to start with his apology for the timing of his bombshell right before I had to do a live broadcast. I remember I wrote, "I treat my co-workers with respect and I expect the same."

Ok this move might've skirted past bold into reckless. This could burn the bridge with this boss, reducing to ashes any chance of advancement while he's at the helm.

I knew my next move would be critically important. I had to go back to work. I had to face the boss. I had to move forward and pull myself together.

For all my mistakes, this I can say I learned to do consistently when I was in the proverbial hole and had to climb out of it.

I dug deep inside to rediscover who I was and what I believed. It's the beginning of being bold.

This process would always take me to Mother Teresa's "Anyway" poem about finding personal meaning in adversity, which was published in *Mother Teresa: A Simple Path*.[5] The poem, which hung on the wall of Mother Teresa's children's home in Calcutta, includes eight of the ten "Paradoxical Commandments" Dr. Kent M. Keith wrote for fellow students when he was a 19 year old sophomore at Harvard College in 1968, coincidentally the year I was born.[12]

ANYWAY

People are unreasonable, illogical and self-centered,

LOVE THEM ANYWAY

If you do good, people will accuse you of selfish,
ulterior motives,

DO GOOD ANYWAY

If you are successful,
you win false friends and true enemies,

SUCCEED ANYWAY

The good you do will be forgotten tomorrow,

DO GOOD ANYWAY

Honesty and frankness make you vulnerable,

BE HONEST AND FRANK ANYWAY

What you spent years building may be
destroyed overnight,

BUILD ANYWAY

People really need help
but may attack you if you help them,

HELP PEOPLE ANYWAY

Give the world the best you have
and you'll get kicked in the teeth,

GIVE THE WORLD THE BEST
YOU'VE GOT ANYWAY.

I have a copy of the "Anyway" poem in my kitchen window at home and kept a copy at my desk at work. The last part of the poem is my go-to when I get kicked in the teeth.

"Give the world the best you have and you'll get kicked in the teeth. Give the world the best you've got anyway.[5]

Reading these words at this moment in which I felt so crushed by my boss got me re-focused on who I was and what I believed. I give my best regardless of whether it's appreciated. I just do it...anyway.

The poem really helped, but it was just the start of my recovery from the "double whammy" I'd just been dealt. I reached out to friends who believe in me. I called my parents for some words of wisdom. And on this occasion I had to pull out the big gun. Barbra Streisand.

If people could only see me dancing around the house to Barbra's "Don't Rain on My Parade!" Don't knock it. It never fails. By the end of that song, I'm ready to "march my band out" and "beat my drum." It worked this time too. The next day I showed up for work with vigor and enthusiasm, ready to do better work than I ever had.

And the boss noticed. Not too long after he delivered that devastating blow I had interpreted as the end of my career, he offered me the coveted morning anchor position. He became one of the biggest cheerleaders of my career.

I've thought a lot since about how this boss handled my strong words as I was so angry with him, and I give him a lot of credit. In the days and weeks that followed, he gave me space to recover. He owned that his timing and delivery missed the mark. He stayed quiet and took the figurative punch to the stomach. God I respect that.

It allowed me to see his perspective, and softened my pain. A good news director leads a busy life that requires quick conversations in a bustling newsroom. If he's doing his job right, he has a lot on the brain. He didn't mean to imply I was a loser when he said he was giving that previous anchor position to someone else, "Because we have to win." The humility he showed in giving me grace made it easier for me to show him what a winner I could be. That's leadership.

Going to the core of what I believed brought *me* to a place of humility as well. Humility is powerful (especially when you have the ego of a news anchor). Daddy used to drum this into my head. He'd remind me, "Humility is the beginning of all good things."

Ego will take you straight to bitterness. Humility will take you to what matters most in the depth of your soul— to why God put you on this Earth, which I believe is to love and serve Him and the people he puts around you. This is my "big picture," my go-to in times of despair.

> *Ego will take you straight to bitterness. Humility will take you to what matters most in the depth of your soul.*

There have been and probably will be times in my life that I've hit the floor, face down, in order to get to this sacred place inside.

No one leads a perfect charmed life. We've all suffered blows. When you're knocked to your knees, you might as well go all the way down to the floor. Then get up, shake off the bitterness like a big coat in South Louisiana heat, and dance around to a Barbra Streisand song or whoever's music does it for you. *All's fair in love and war*, especially when the war is within yourself.

Soothe that frightened little girl or boy inside however you can. Then "march that band out" with all the positivity you can muster, and have some fun. You'll eventually get the respect you want, and it's just a good way to live.

CHAPTER 11

LET'S ROCK THE BOAT BABY

Will We Sink or Swim?

Y ou've seen the gaffes and technical snafus.

Sometimes it's anything but smooth sailing in live local TV news, and in this business, the bad moments are out there for the world to see.

The last thing you want to do is make waves that could cause one of these credibility busters.

But sometimes in live television, a bold move is the right move. Even if it sends your manager into a screaming, F-bomb hurling fit of rage.

Yep. That happened.

More than 27 years now into my career in 2018, I had recently been moved from weekends to anchor the morning news solo in Cincinnati. The whole morning show team was feeling the pressure to climb in the ratings, namely our fiercely aggressive, no nonsense executive producer (E.P.).

Julie O'Neill has fun behind the scenes as WCPO morning show anchor with Jaclyn D'Augustino and Ryan Houston in 2018.

Scripts got written tight, the talent hit time marks, and the directors kept pace rolling video and graphics or we'd hear it from this E.P., and it wouldn't be in Dale Carnegie's *How to Win Friends and Influence People* language. Her rough edges brought the producers working under her to tears on a fairly frequent basis. One of my roles on the team was to wipe those tears, while trying to coax this E.P. into a gentler style of communication. Sometimes this was as challenging as my on-air anchor duties.

Yes, the anchor does more than read from a teleprompter.

The term "anchor" for a newscaster is a reference to the most important player on a sports team such as the last runner on a relay team, key to winning the race. Though Walter Cronkite was not the first man in TV to be referred to as an anchorman, he brought new meaning to the term as he was covering the 1952 Democratic and Republican conventions for CBS, because he took charge of which reporters to go to and when.[13] Everyone followed his lead.

In a typical newscast today, the anchor is mostly following a script and the executive producer (E.P.) is the manager in charge of the newscast, but in dynamic situations, the anchor has to take the lead in guiding the show. You can see how there could sometimes be some tension between an anchor and an E.P.

So here's what I did that awakened the ire of my E.P. as no one thought was possible until that fateful day.

It was the morning we were reporting on the impending White House visit of one of our local sheriffs. Butler County Sheriff Richard Jones had a strong reputation for being outspoken in his county north of Cincinnati. It was a big deal that he would have the ear of then President Donald Trump that afternoon. Ideally we would've had an interview with Sheriff Jones about what he planned to do and say, but let's just say he didn't care much for my station. Our competitors would have interviews with him, but our reporter on the story that morning was going to have to say, "We reached out to the Sheriff for comment, but have not heard back yet." Ugh. I hated that. That's not how to win a race!

I decided to take matters into my own hands. While Sheriff Jones didn't much like my station, he and I always had a good working relationship, so much so that he trusted me with his cell phone number.

Butler County Sheriff Richard K. Jones (Courtesy: Richard Jones)

I figured the good sheriff would be up pretty early to catch his flight to Washington D.C., so sometime after 5:00 a.m., as I was in the midst of anchoring the newscast, I shot the sheriff a text during a commercial break.

"Hey Sheriff, you up and moving yet on your big day? Any chance you'll give me a quick comment about going to meet with the president today?"

Minutes passed. More minutes passed. No response as the newscast continued on. *Boy, I really thought he would text me back*, I thought. *Oh well, It was worth a try.*

Then suddenly, I looked down at my vibrating cell phone on the news desk.

Sheriff Jones was *calling* me!

Didn't anticipate that. I was just hoping for a short statement in a text. We were in a commercial break, so I answered my phone. I hoped to get a quick statement from the sheriff before we came back on the air.

So much for that.

After hello's and such, time had run out. We were back on the air and the weather person was giving her mini forecast a few feet away from me in the studio. I had not yet gotten a statement from the sheriff, and in about 30 seconds, we were set to broadcast the story about his trip that day to Washington.

I found myself faced with a dilemma. I could just hang up with the sheriff and keep the show as scripted. That would be the safe move. But here was the problem with that. The reporter on the story about the sheriff's trip was scripted to say that we had not heard back from him. I knew that was no longer true. I had him on my cell phone at that very moment. He *had* gotten back to us.

So should I let this reporter give our viewers inaccurate information, and blow off the sheriff who took time to call me?

Or should I rock the boat?

You knew this was coming.

I rocked the boat.

Now just so you know, I wouldn't have done this if I didn't think my plan would work and everyone involved was up to the task. When a bold move involves risk for other people, you have to measure it more carefully, keeping everyone on your team in mind. A quarterback doesn't call an audible that he doesn't think his team can execute.

When a bold move involves risk for other people, you have to measure it more carefully, keeping everyone on your team in mind.

Ok, here we go, I thought, as my heart started thumping a little faster.

The weather person was wrapping up her mini forecast, so I had to be quiet in the studio.

I whispered to the sheriff, "You ok with me putting you live on the air?"

"Sure," he said.

"Ok, hold on a sec," I told him.

As the camera came to me live on the set, I was holding up my cell phone and immediately announced, "I'll tell you I now have on the phone Butler County Sheriff Richard Jones just returning my call…"

I went on to follow the script in the teleprompter, telling the viewers about the sheriff's plans to meet with the president.

Then, I put the Sheriff on speaker phone, as I held my cell phone next to the microphone clipped onto my blouse.

"Sheriff Jones?" I said, to make sure he was still there.

"Yes ma'am," he answered.

The audio from my cell phone sounded perfect on the air. *Great!*

"We got you. You're live on Good Morning Tristate," I said.

"Before we go to Breanna Molly live in the studio with more on today's meeting, anything you want to say about this meeting and your chance to speak with President Trump?"

Our conversation took off. The sheriff was excited about his trip, and was as engaging and colorful as ever. This was working.

There was no graphic to put on the screen, because a producer would need advance notice to create one of those. The viewers just saw me holding my cell phone up to my mic. I knew to keep it short and simple.

As I said goodbye to the sheriff, I then had to transition to the reporter, Breanna, to detail the sheriff's schedule for the day.

Breanna had been listening, as a good reporter does. She tweaked her script to transition from my interview and skip past the sentence in the teleprompter about the sheriff not getting back to us yet.

Jim, who was running the teleprompter, had been paying close attention too. He scrolled up quickly to keep up with where Breanna was in the script.

Peter, the director, was also on his game. He kept the camera on me for my call with the sheriff, then picked right up with the video and graphics needed as Breanna gave her report.

No technical implosions, and we got the sheriff on the air! It was great live television! Kudos to the anchor, right?!

Oh mercy! If you could've been there as the E.P. came charging into the studio during the next commercial break. "What the F___?!!!" She shouted at me. As I can best recollect, that was followed by a "Don't you ever..." and an "I'm in charge..."

Boy was she mad. She ripped me up one side and down the other. It was stunning, even for her.

Perhaps just as shocking to my co-workers who witnessed the E.P.'s tirade was my silence, though. After the show, one of my co-workers asked me how I could just sit there and take that. I explained to her that once a woman enters her fifties, if she's developed any maturity at all, she knows the difference between being a doormat and displaying quiet strength. I knew this considerably younger E.P. was frustrated and out of control at that moment. I've been there. Sometimes it's better to defer conversations when cooler heads can prevail. Anyway, it was pretty easy since I knew I was right. And the E.P. would figure it out soon enough when the big boss, the news director, came into work. I knew he was going to love what I did.

The big boss did love it. And so did the other members of the morning team, who had to adjust when I went off script.

Breanna, the reporter, said she was glad she hadn't been set up to say something that was untrue.

Peter, the director, told me that following my lead that morning was the most fun he'd had in a long time.

They both thought getting the sheriff live on the air was "so cool!"

So did the rest of the news team.

Our website team immediately pulled the clip from the show and posted it for the world to see. When the dayside reporters arrived at the station for their shift, several came over to my desk to give me an atta girl. One remarked, "That's the best live television I've seen on our air in weeks!"

No one had ever thought to put a cell phone up to a microphone, when time didn't permit us to do things the traditional way. Other anchors used my little trick after that.

There are reasons for best practices. Good reasons. In TV news, we need to have good, clean shows, free of hiccups that are jarring to viewers. We need to be respected as professionals to protect our credibility. But in a competitive business, a bold move in a dynamic situation can take you to the next level and set you apart from the rest. You just have to measure the risks.

In a competitive business, a bold move in a dynamic situation can take you to the next level and set you apart from the rest.

On this day, in this case, I'd made the right call for my crew, rocking the boat. We did something fresh and different and the result was a better product for our customers, our viewers.

And my E.P. got over it. We're all in a learning process in this crazy life. She's a big talent and a rising star in the business. A glass of wine together that Friday night and we were friends again. That's broadcast news.

CHAPTER 12

HANG ON HONEY, MOMMA'S GOTTA WORK

Bring Your Daughter to a SWAT Scene Day

I f you're a true news dog, your sniffer never shuts off. The waft of a good story will perk your head up at any time of day. Sometimes the alert you get that it's time to give chase comes as you're already in your bathrobe and slippers for the night. Your family knows this. And sometimes they know they're going to come along for the hunt.

One such adventure unfolded on a cold winter day in the latter part of my career, when my daughter was a freshman in high school. She had a club meeting after school, so that meant a late pick up. And that meant Momma was going to greet her in her bathrobe and slippers. Hey, I was anchoring early mornings at that time. The alarm went off at 2:00 a.m. No apologies. I mean, all I had to do was pull up to the front circle of the school, let my daughter hop in the car, and drive straight home. Right?

Well on this day, my daughter pulled open the car door with an apology for taking so long to come out. "Sorry, Mom, they made us all go back to the cafeteria for our safety," she said. "Apparently there's some SWAT situation going on around here somewhere."

"What's this?" I asked, my head perking up in signature news dog style.

"Where? Tell me exactly what the teachers said."

"I don't know, Mom. Something about the hotel down the street," she answered.

My daughter knew the hunt was on.

"Buckle up baby," I said. With a smile and an eye roll, my teenager cocked her seat back a little, pulled a book out of her bag, and resigned herself that Momma was going to work for a while. And dinner was going to be served late.

As we pulled out of the school parking lot to head to the hotel, I noticed a cop car go behind a big office building set back and hidden from the main road. No lights and sirens, but it was from a jurisdiction on the other side of town. *What is this guy doing over here, and where is he going?* I thought. We followed him. Of course.

Not thirty seconds later, jackpot! We see police cars from several jurisdictions. Guys are suiting up. They're pulling big guns out of trunks. There was no other news media there. Just me. *Oh hell yes!* I thought.

This was just the staging area where the SWAT team was organizing, and the hotel was a block away, so my daughter was not in any danger. Still, I parked the car at a distance, and told my daughter to keep her head down.

"I'll be right back," I told my daughter.

"Ok Mom, I'll just be reading my book," she mumbled unimpressed, while giving me the side eye about what I was wearing.

No I didn't approach the scene in my bathrobe and slippers, although that might've made for a better story. I always kept jackets and several pairs of shoes in the car. Girl Scout mentality. I also kept a microphone plug-in for my cell phone in the slot of my car door.

I quickly changed into suitable attire, hit record on my cell phone and rolled video as I made my way toward the activity. This is how I had watched crack photographer Chic Poppe get all the best video back in the day. He rolled first, and asked forgiveness later. It's not the right thing to do in every situation, but it worked for this one.

A spokesperson for the police immediately approached me and she answered questions as I videotaped. A suspect was holed up in that hotel my daughter had mentioned. It was a block away from us. She asked me to blur the faces of SWAT team members before my video made air. I of course agreed. Some were undercover guys.

"Is the Chief here?" I asked the spokesperson. I told her I had interviewed him a couple of weeks ago about the department's "Stuff the Cruiser" toy drive. "Will you tell him Julie O'Neill is here?" I asked, "And ask him if I can ride along for the arrest?"

While the police spokesperson checked with the chief, it was back to the car for me, to check on my daughter and warm myself while I texted the video back to the news station.

The evening news was in full swing. No competing news outlet knew a thing about the SWAT situation that would soon be shutting down roads and evacuating a large hotel. I was on the front end of this thing. I had the scoop! Quickly, I typed the info into my cell phone and alerted the team. I sent them video after video, with instructions to blur faces. I also texted the anchors, who were live on the set, that breaking news was coming. We anchors know to take care of each other.

The newsroom was scrambling, content coordinators editing my video, producers re-stacking their newscasts. "You're a rockstar, Julie!" One of the managers messaged back.

My daughter continued to read, lifting her head up from her book only to ask, "How much longer are we going to be out here Mom? I'm hungry."

My station worked to redirect a reporter and photographer to the SWAT scene to relieve me. They knew it was now past my bedtime. In the meantime, I kept shooting video as I texted updates to the anchors on the set, who were now delivering the breaking news with my exclusive interview. What fun! And the best was yet to come.

The spokesperson for the police walked over to me with some good news and bad news. "The Chief says you can't come with the SWAT team over to the hotel. Too dangerous. But..." she went on. And wait till you hear this. "The Chief said he'll shoot video of the arrest with his cell phone, and text it to you."

He said WHAT?! I thought. *Did I just hear this woman say the Chief of Police was going to shoot a video for me?!* I about had the big one. I always had a good rapport with law enforcement, but this was a first.

I had just met this Chief for the first time a couple of weeks before to interview him about his department's toy drive. The police station was on my way home from work, so I made the quick stop and he and I had time to chat a bit afterward. We talked about the toy drive and how that was as uplifting for his officers as it was for the kids getting the toys. We talked about how being a part of good and positive things was important for police, who see so much bad. It wasn't a super long or deep conversation, but it was a good one.

As the conversation with this Chief ended, I told him I wanted him to have my cell phone number, so he could easily shoot me a text when his department had something good to share that might be newsworthy. I also asked him for his cell phone number, promising I would never abuse it or give it to anyone else without his consent.

This is something I did with pretty much everybody I interviewed. You never know whom you might need to contact with a follow up question or reach out to on a related matter. People didn't mind giving me their cell phone number, particularly when I gave them mine. I wanted them to be able to reach me quickly in case I missed something or got a detail wrong in their story. This would help them help me protect the accuracy of their story, which these days lives forever on the internet. I also wanted them to have my number for future reference in case they might come across other news, and encouraged them to call or text if they did. Some of my best tips and important exclusives came from everyday people to whom I'd given my cell phone number.

Asking a public figure, like a police chief, for a personal cell phone number required a little more boldness. All they can say is no. If you want to be a bolder person, you have to make friends with the word "no," and get comfortable with the awkwardness that comes with it. In the case of this Chief, the risk of an awkward moment was worth the payoff. A couple of weeks later, he was promising to shoot the video of an arrest for me!

If you want to be a bolder person, you have to make friends with the word "no," and get comfortable with the awkwardness that comes with it.

Anyway, this word from the spokesperson about the Chief's generous offer had my heart racing. I ran back to the car, threw open the driver's side door, and shouted the huge news to my daughter.

Kind enough to take a pause from her reading and effort a half smile, she answered, "Oh that's good, Mom."

She then continued with, " Are we almost done then? I'm really getting hungry."

We were almost done. The crew coming to replace me arrived shortly thereafter. Minutes later I had the video of the arrest shot by the Chief. Just for me. I fired the exclusive video off to the station, and my daughter and I were homeward bound for dinner.

———◇———

If you ever need your ego shrunk back down to a tolerable size, you can always count on your teenager for help. It's just not in their nature to swoon over a parent's success. But I do think it's a good thing for a daughter to see her mother being bold, and working hard in her passion.

And I did eventually get my daughter to admit she enjoyed "Take Your Daughter to a SWAT Scene Day." She had a great story to tell her friends and teachers the day after. They were eating it up at lunch as she shared how, while everyone else was hunkered down, she was in the action. Though she hated to admit it, she was proud to have a news dog for a Momma.

Julie O'Neill and her ever patient teen daughter (2021)

CHAPTER 13

THE NOT SO GRAND FINALE

How I Got Kicked off the Stage

I wrestled with this chapter. I wrestled, not just with what to include, but with whether to include it at all.

The primary purpose of this book is to inspire boldness in you, based on my realization that boldness was the common thread woven through every key story of success and survival over my long career. I wrestled with this final chapter because it doesn't offer the dramatic finish to my TV news career that I imagined for myself.

That said, I told you in the introduction of this book that my best girlfriends aka my "Board of Directors" insisted I could not write a book about the importance of being bold, and not be bold enough to speak about the crushing twist at the end of my storied career in TV news. They said I had to flip on the floodlight and show what lurks in the dark in my business and others, so that maybe, just maybe, I could make a difference for others as I forge ahead with my future. Just know that this chapter is not the last chapter. Promising things are happening. I promise.

Well here goes.

My exit from broadcast news began as I was making my 55th trip around the sun, and the sun was shining. I wasn't at my "power weight" of younger years, but I looked good and felt squarely in my prime. I was bringing the mojo to the set as the morning anchor, turning the enterprising stories, and mentoring the younger reporters like a rock star.

The start of 2022 was an exciting time to be doing news in Cincinnati. The Bengals, led by Joe Burrow, had the Queen City lit up. Comeback Joe had recovered from that nasty injury in his first season as a Bengal, and now in his second season had driven our team to the playoffs.

Joe doesn't know me from Adam's house cat (as my brother would put it) but he and I had quite a history. I was brought up in Baton Rouge where most of my family still lives. Proud LSU alum. A couple of years before, in 2019, as my father was making his final drive to the goal line to be with God, Baton Rouge was on fire with "Burreaux" fever. I watched every game from my Loveland, Ohio home, cheering along with the family down in the Bayou State on a group text.

As Joe's triumphant final collegiate season was unfolding, my dad, who was captain of LSU's golf team in his day, was cheering on Joe from the hospital and eventually his quiet room in hospice care. I flew down to be with him in his final days. For two nights, I slept on the pullout couch chair in his hospice room. I remember lying there listening to him breathe all night, like I had done years before with my newborn babies. When there was any interruption to his breath, I immediately sat up, my body clinched, awaiting the sound of his breath again. It was intense. He hung on. I had to leave him and return to Cincinnati to work.

We lost dad within a few days of me saying goodbye to him. It was just before LSU's big game against Alabama, which meant putting off the service for two weekends. No one in Baton Rouge was going to go to a funeral on the Saturday of the big Alabama game. Heck, we didn't want to miss the game either. It's an odd feeling to be grieving the death of your father, while also wanting to cheer on your football team, but that's what we did, as we envisioned Dad leading the cheering section in heaven.

I watched the game at O'Bryon's Bar and Grill in Cincinnati, shouting along with a table full of LSU alums, as the family cheered on Joe Burrow down in Baton Rouge, where it seemed like signs filled every storefront and purple and gold ribbons wrapped every light pole. My mother became so anxious watching the game at a party, she walked outside to sit in her car and calm her nerves, but could still hear the shouts and screams emanating from houses all along the street. There was no escaping the excitement.

I give you my "history" with Joe Burrow to show you the impact he had on me long before he became a Cincinnati Bengal. I'd seen the hope and inspiration he'd brought to Baton Rouge. I'd seen the joy he'd brought my ever-competitive father in his final days. I'd seen how these things had brought comfort to my grieving family.

When it became clear the Cincinnati Bengals were going to have a shot at getting Joe Burrow as their first-round draft pick, I was lit up! "This city is about to change," I told everyone in the newsroom. There were naysayers during Joe's first season with the Bengals, but no losses nor no injury would sway my belief in him.

Suffice it to say I was well known as the loudest Burrow/Bengals cheerleader on and off the air at work as Joe's second Bengals season started showing momentum, now with LSU's Ja'Marr Chase to hurl his jaw-dropping passes to. Colleagues texted me during and after each game. They chuckled at my excitement, which fueled laughter and enthusiasm at the office on Monday mornings.

That's why some questioned why I wasn't picked to go to Tennessee to cover the Bengals' first playoff game for the morning show I was anchoring. The bosses sent my co-anchor. I shook that off but made clear I wanted to go to the next playoff game in Kansas City against the Chiefs. My co-anchor was picked to go to that game too.

Now I felt nervous, and anxious. I got very direct with my brand new news director and my long time general manager that I wanted to go to Los Angeles to cover the Super Bowl. I made my case as the obvious choice. I had followed the Bengals for almost 27 years as an anchor/reporter at this station. I knew the history and what this moment meant. I had felt the deep disappointments of Bengals losses along with the fans in Cincinnati over the years, and I would certainly bring the authentic enthusiasm live on scene. My co-anchor, Adrian, was a great talent, but he was new to the city.

"You're on the short list," my news director told me, "We'll let you know when we decide who goes."

When I learned that the bosses picked Adrian to do our morning show coverage in Los Angeles for the Super Bowl, it was a gut punch. There's no overstating it.

Let me be clear. My co-anchor, Adrian, was and is one of the finest human beings I know. A Marine. A stand up guy who doesn't hold back when he smells a rat, and the first to go toe-to-toe with anyone who gets it wrong or God forbid mistreats someone. It's a great blessing to have a partner you admire both personally and professionally. I certainly had no ill feelings toward Adrian. He didn't ask for that assignment, but wasn't going to say no, nor should he.

For me this decision signaled something much bigger than the disappointment of not being there in L.A. with Joe and the Bengals. It told me that it didn't matter how long or hard I worked, how many exclusives I got, how much I could add to the team through my longtime contacts in the community, or how much enthusiasm I brought to the job. I was no longer a first string player in *my* game. The bosses did not see me as the future.

Please understand, I know from my series of reports on the struggle to get unemployment benefits during the pandemic, just how bad some people have it. I'm very much in touch with how abundantly blessed I've been in comparison. Still, my pressures are my own. Here I was a 54-year-old single mom with one income keeping the world turning in my household, and that was mine. All I'd known was that if I worked hard and went above and beyond, it always paid off. Now the reality was setting in that my world was about to spin off its axis, and there was nothing I could do about it. I felt helpless, and I felt scared.

I reached out to my union representative for advice. He too was shocked I had been passed over for every preferred assignment in the Bengals march to football's grand finale. He suggested that he be the one to take the concern to the station's general manager. He asked my GM pointedly whether my age, sex or color had anything to do with his decision.

The response from the general manager was "no." He said that the main evening anchor, Tanya, and I were the "faces of the station," and he could not have both of us gone to L.A. for the Super Bowl at the same time. He said if the Bengals lost the big game, Cincinnati fans would want to wake up in the morning to Julie O'Neill on the news set for comfort.

I found that sell hard to buy, but I accepted it and went about making the best contribution I could to the Super Bowl coverage with and for the fans watching from Cincinnati. It was the only thing to do.

Julie O'Neill anchors Bengals Super Bowl coverage in 2022.

I searched for, found, shot, edited and reported some great feature content in addition to my regular duties as the morning anchor. I used my contacts and historic knowledge of the Bengals to help set up my co-anchor for success in L.A. I felt sure my continued enthusiasm and extra effort leading up to the Super Bowl would show the bosses I was bigger than their decision. But everything was different from then till the end.

The general manager seemed to dodge me in the months that followed. He didn't come around my desk or speak to me as he'd done before. The new news director largely ignored me at first, and then the cold criticism started regarding my on-air performance. I was saying "uh" too much. I was stumbling too much in my ad libs. I was laughing too much. My tosses weren't good. And so on. There was no mention of my good moments on the air, and even when I got all the gang to laugh at something in the morning post-show meetings, I got scowls and glares from him.

The contempt for me was palpable. I continued to try harder to smooth things over, turning a lot of enterprising content. That's when the reporter goes out and finds stories no one else is doing. Usually in the news business that's highly valued. Nothing helped.

I was eventually called into a disciplinary meeting, with the station's head of human resources present, during which the news director accused me of not taking his performance issues with me seriously. He said I had not made the changes and improvements he'd asked for.

I sat there in disbelief. I had been recording and watching my newscasts, noting my tosses to reporters, any stumbles, and even how often I laughed. As self-critical as I can be, I just didn't see what he was talking about. I assured him I took everything he said seriously.

I wisely had my union representative present at the disciplinary meeting. Afterward, he told me he was baffled. As we stood outside the station near our cars, I remember the dazed look in his eyes as he shook his head. He said he'd never seen an anchor called up to human resources for something like this. *Performance issues with a 30-year news veteran has become a disciplinary issue?* "Clearly they're gunning for you," he said.

The meeting had ended with a warning that my performance would be watched closely for improvement, and we would all meet back to discuss it in a month.

My co-anchor, Adrian, called to check on me later that afternoon. I had told him about the impending meeting. Co-anchors often spend more time with each other than their spouses or closest friends. There's no hiding it when something big is going on. I filled him in. I felt the heaviness of his heart as he struggled for what to say.

The next day on the set as the morning show was about to start, Adrian tried a little humor to ease the pressure he had to know I was feeling. "No problem, Julie," he said. "Just be perfect for the next month. No ad libs. Don't try to fix the problems with the copy. Just read what's in the teleprompter. No stumbles. Piece of cake." We did both have a good laugh at that. Nothing like the pressure of being perfect. The red light below the camera lit up, and I did the best I could.

It was *rinse and repeat* for the next few weeks. Continual self-talk. *You can do this. No mistakes,* I told myself. The hardest part was wondering what was true from my bosses, and what was a legal maneuver to build a case to get rid of me. *Have I lost my edge? Am I not the talent I once was? Was I ever talented?* It's one thing to not feel wanted. It's another to feel you're not good at what you do.

Even under the pressure of perfection each day, while trying to anchor a fun and engaging morning show, I managed to keep my performance almost flub-free. I'd elbow Adrian when he had a gaffe as he was reading over video, earning a smile from him. And when I made a small blunder, it was all I could do not to burst out laughing when I'd see him in my peripheral vision tense up with big eyes. He kept me laughing and propped me up with genuine encouragement during this intense time. I love him for that.

Anchor Adrian Whitsett holds back laughter on the set (2022).

Despite my best efforts, that call up to human resources (HR) would come. This time it was the general manager (GM) calling for a meeting, the news director's boss. He texted me on a Monday, my final day off of a long weekend, that he wanted to meet with me about the issues the news director had brought to HR. His texts stated that I was not to come in to anchor the morning show the next day, but rather I was to come up to his office to meet with him and the head of HR at 10:00 a.m.

Well here it was. I was either going to be suspended or fired. What did they have on me? It seemed to me my reads and tosses had been super clean since the meeting with my news director and head of HR, now more than a month before.

I racked my brain. This didn't make sense. A friend suggested I make a list of anything and everything I could've possibly done to warrant this, and prepare responses. I struggled to come up with anything. The previous night as I was attending a fundraiser, I ran into Ohio's secretary of state, so using my cell phone, I grabbed a quick interview with him about the upcoming election and texted it to the station. *Had I said or done something inappropriate in that interview?*

I called one of the reporters at my station and found out she used my interview in her reports that morning, and the team was pumped to have it, so that couldn't be it. I spent the whole day and night trying to think of what I could've possibly done wrong, preparing for the blade of the chopping block to drop on my neck the next morning.

At 10 a.m. on September 13, 2022, I walked into a small conference room where my GM, the station's HR rep, and my union rep were waiting for me. Some awkward small talk wrapped up among the three of them, as I sat down stoically. My general manager began reading a letter about my "failure to follow direction and unacceptable professional conduct." The beginning of the letter he read summarized the most recent incident, which had happened eleven days prior on September 2nd.

I listened to my GM read...

"At the top of the 5am show, you told the audience about an employee's medical condition live on air when tossing to her for the weather. This caused the employee to fumble over her words and put the employee in an uncomfortable situation. Discussing another employee's personal medical information publicly without her consent is disrespectful and unprofessional, particularly live on air."

I felt like I was having an out of body experience. I couldn't believe what I was hearing.

The *employee* to whom the letter refers had announced on social media in the week leading up to September 2nd that she had covid. "COVID finally got me!" was the headline on her Facebook page. While this *employee* was out sick for the week, she went live on Instagram twice, discussing every detail of her covid symptoms, along with who gave her the virus and how so many of her neighbors had covid as well. The first Instagram post was over eight minutes long. The second post was over ten minutes long. Nothing was left out. At one point she stated, "I have nothing to hide as you guys know. I never hide anything when it comes to my life." Links to her Instagram live interactions were shared to her Facebook page, which had some 50,000 followers. So many people apparently saw her social media posts, I had people approach me that week at the grocery store and other public places and ask me how this *employee* was doing in her recovery from covid.

Given all this, it seemed perfectly natural and appropriate to ask the *employee* about it when welcoming her back to work, and give her a moment to let viewers know how she was feeling. It had been drummed into our heads during recent anchor training that viewers wanted real and genuine interactions. I certainly would not have mentioned her covid had she not previously revealed it so openly and comfortably with tens of thousands of social media followers, many of whom were probably watching the news that morning.

The exchange on the air between this *employee*, my co-anchor and me felt genuine and friendly, and I thought it demonstrated that the team cares about each other. The *employee* seemed very comfortable having her moment, so when she called me out during the next commercial break for mentioning her covid recovery, I was stunned and confused. I immediately apologized and tried to explain my intention. Someone else in the studio apparently saw no basis for her beef and interjected, "This is bullshit!"

The response from my immediate managers seemed to mirror that sentiment. One remarked that more people probably knew the *employee* had covid from her social media than were watching at 5 o'clock in the morning. Another later remarked, "She uses social media to get attention," as he rolled his eyes about her covid posts. That's why it was so shocking to me that this was something the GM decided to use as a justification to discipline me for being "disrespectful" and "unprofessional."

When the GM finished reading the entire letter, he looked up and said that I was being taken off the morning show effective immediately, and that my contract (ending in less than 4 months) would not be renewed. Then he spelled out my options for the remaining months of my contract. He said I could work as a reporter for the last few months of my contract, or I could leave now and be paid through the end of my contract.

I stayed quiet, as what the GM had read from the letter repeated in my head. The loudest phrases were those toward the end of the letter about how my "behavior" was "incredibly concerning to the team" and "created reputational risk for the team, for the show, and for the station."

My response was visceral. I felt like I was shaking and paralyzed all at once. *Is he talking about ME?* I thought. That was just so opposite of who I believed I was and have always been. It was like nothing in the world made sense anymore.

I left quietly. I stayed very quiet for days, just processing all of this, and praying. My reaction would matter. My family and friends would watch to see how I handled this. The public would too. I wanted to get it right.

Following the announcement of my departure after 27 years doing TV news in Cincinnati, I was overwhelmed by the response from the public. There was great support and encouragement, which was comforting and healing. And there was tremendous outrage. Though no explanation was given about why I was suddenly gone from the air without a goodbye, it was as though the reason was obvious to everyone. I was inundated with messages from people, saying something similar had happened to them or someone they knew. It seemed apparent to all that the great offense which led to my termination was that I dared to get older.

Nine days after the end of my final contract, I would turn 55, officially casting me out of the all important TV news age 18-54 audience demographic.

Let that sink in.

———◇———

It's a strange thing. You blink. And suddenly you could be everyone's mother at the office. Some of the reporters I mentored even affectionately called me "Momma J." It's a wonderful time of life to be in the position to encourage the up and comers, and to have the know-how to help them. You cherish those moments they hang on your every word as you dispense some wisdom for what they're going through. It's galvanizing to see them grow an inch taller as a suggestion you share brings them success. You relish the role of welcoming in and building up the next generation.

In quiet moments alone, though, a woman in her fifties wonders when "the newer" is going to displace "the older."

It's incredulous to me that in this day and age women my age have to worry about this. That some see us as having nothing left to offer.

We're Sandra Bullock, Queen Latifah, Brene Brown, and Shonda Rhimes. Strong. Beautiful. Bold women taking care of ourselves, and often taking care of our kids and our parents while we're at it.

This is why I feel the need to be bold here on behalf of the women, and yes some men too, who've had a similar experience to mine. We have to question the *why* of these terminations.

I should note that my decision to raise questions with candor in this book came at a cost. My former employer held me to a one-year non-compete agreement, which prohibited me from anchoring or reporting for other news outlets where I live, regardless of the reason for my termination. There would be no reduction in the time frame I was locked out from work, nor any severance pay from my former employer, unless I signed a non-disclosure agreement (NDA). I would have to give up my right to speak openly, own my story, and share my opinions on the company's actions for the rest of my life.

My decision to forgo the money in favor of maintaining my right to free speech may not be the right one for everyone, but it was the right one for me. After much prayer and contemplation, I came to the realization that I just didn't have it in me to give a company control over what I can and can not say. I kept thinking about all the people who have given their lives and fortunes to give me this freedom. How blessed am I to have it! My best friend says this is the boldest thing I've ever done. I told her maybe I was put in this position because I'm just crazy enough to push away the cash on the premise that one small voice can make a difference.

And it's not just the *why* of my termination that concerns me, but also the *how*.

Here were managers working to convince me that I was an incompetent discipline problem. And all of this happened under the watchful eyes of corporate leaders, who'd called on me years before to head the leadership training for my Station.

Some like to say, "It's just business. It's not personal." I say all of business is personal, because it involves people. It's the prerogative of businesses to end contracts. Sometimes tough decisions must be made and people have varying opinions about the value of workers. That's fair game. But do we really believe it's an acceptable legal maneuver to diminish an employee's self worth, and instill fear in the workplace?

> *Some like to say, "It's just business. It's not personal." I say all of business is personal, because it involves people.*

In my view, a true company leader doesn't allow managers to play mind games, while looking the other way, hiding behind lawyers. A true, courageous leader stands up and respects people, while respecting the bottom line.

Please don't mistake my need to speak up as something rooted in bitterness. Sure I felt some at first, but I very quickly set an intention to release it. I know it's a poison that hardens the heart and otherwise wreaks havoc on the whole body. I think the key for me to ridding myself of bitterness was embracing the grieving process, which was an interesting time for me.

Denial…anger…bargaining…depression…

The turning point for me came one Saturday after all the drama of my departure had settled. Something happened to hit a button inside me. And I had a good, long, intense cry. Then a couple of hours later I had another. Then a few hours after that I had yet another. I remember being surprised amid the third bout of tears that there was any more left inside. It wasn't a sad cry. It was a release of all the pressure I had felt in this job I so loved. For more than 30 years my life was chasing stories, racing toward deadlines, sweating contract negotiations, working to keep my weight down and otherwise find the right clothes and makeup to look good, fresh, and up to date, day after day on the air. It was over now. That part of my life was over.

What I later came to understand about that Saturday of tears is that it was the tail end of the grieving process. I had reflected on what I had lost and let it go. It was the day I got to the other side. I had arrived at the final stage of grief, *acceptance.*

On the last day I would ever walk into the building I worked in for so many years, I was escorted into the newsroom by the news director to clean out my desk. He stayed in his office as, one by one, my co-workers came over to offer hugs and kind words. Such great people. It was surreal, but there was a peace about it for me. I kept looking up at the panel of my cubicle where Mother Teresa's "Anyway" poem hung with a push pin. I zeroed in on the last part in particular, that had reminded me throughout my career how to approach a meaningful life.

"Give the world the best you have and you'll get kicked in the teeth. Give the world the best you've got anyway."[5]

I left the poem hanging there for the next person at my desk to see, and with my head held high, I quietly left the newsroom, rolling out two big suitcases full of clothes and makeup, and a cart full of boxes filled with other personal belongings.

Hey, sometimes a bold move doesn't work out so well. I got kicked in the teeth, but I gave the best I had. I had a helluva ride in TV news, boldly pursuing stories that changed laws and touched lives. And I exited stage right with the admiration of those I admire the most.

I offer this book as I transition now to a fresh new stage of life. I'm no longer bound by the journalistic necessity of neutrality, or confined by contractual requirements to keep quiet.

Oh mercy! I stand on the precipice of so many possibilities, as I craft a new career, free to offer my value and creativity on my own terms as a speaker and author.

Who knows what I'll say, or what I'll write in the days, months, and years ahead?

As my bold journey continues, one thing you can surely count on is the continual sound of shattering glass. That'll be me, crashing through my comfort zone. Again.

CHAPTER 14

YOUR PATH FORWARD

You Were Born for Such a Time as This

Esther 4:14

THIS is my time. THIS can be your time as well. We all have unique gifts and talents. I believe those unique gifts are at the heart of anyone and everyone's ability to bring boldness to work and life.

Throughout my broadcast news career, I suppose I knew I brought courage to the job, but it was afterward that I started to dissect what boldness was, how I came to have it, and how other people can get it. I looked at my upbringing. I looked at how I have approached key moments in life, some of which I've now shared with you, and how those turned out. I've also studied the stories of some of our boldest newsmakers, with an eye toward how they brought boldness to their endeavors.

I'd like to leave you with what I believe are the five stepping stones on the footbridge to bold.

#1. Know What You Believe

Find Your Big Picture

I've shared in this book that I believe I was put on this Earth to love and serve God, and the people He puts around me. This is my big picture. It's my go-to for perspective. It's like seeing myself and my problem from outer space, so it helps to clarify where I fit into the world and how this decision I'm facing fits into what I believe about myself and my purpose. It also makes problems seem smaller. I'm a flawed human being capable of teetering on hypocrisy now and again, but I do my best to keep an eye from the sky on what I believe and value. Look at any strong, successful leader who boldly went where others didn't dare. These are people who know what they believe.

Create a Big Picture Statement

Companies spend a lot of time crafting mission statements, as they set their goals and otherwise make business decisions. I suggest you put in writing your "big picture" statement, a go-to reminder of what you believe, and what you exist to do for this world. You are the CEO of your own company, YOU. Invest some time into your business. If you really know what you believe about who you are and what your purpose is, your decisions are simpler to make. The clearer you are about what you believe, the bolder you'll be.

Questions to Ponder:

What do you value most in life?

Can you list the top 10 things you value?

What would a draft of your "big picture" statement look like?

(Remember, these values and your "big picture" statement may evolve as you do.)

#2. Know Yourself

Discover your uniqueness

We live in a time where we can take any number of personality tests online to learn more about ourselves. Our strengths. Our weaknesses. How we show up in the room. There's the Myers-Briggs, the DISC, the Big Five. My personal favorite is the Enneagram, which places everyone into one of nine types of people. I'm a 3 with a strong 4 wing. This means I'm primarily "the performer" with a strong "independent" side that can get very soulful.

Learning the details of my "type" has been invaluable in helping me to understand why I operate the way I do and how to mitigate any negative tendencies. Self awareness and self discovery are so important in our journey to bringing our best authentic selves into the world. Knowing our wiring enables us to own who we are, which brings forth the boldness within us.

Own your uniqueness

Once you really know yourself, own it. Own everything that sets you apart.

I did only a couple of ambush interviews during my career. You've seen these in TV News, where the reporter sneaks up on someone accused of doing something wrong and starts firing questions. Some reporters love these. I didn't. I dreaded having to do them, because I'm wired to want everyone to feel comfortable and happy at all times. Surprisingly though, the outcome of my ambushes was always better than expected.

I found myself in the midst of these uncomfortable situations continually going back to my nature to lighten the heaviness in the room, and make the person I was interviewing feel good again. Sometimes I even joked around with the person. As it turned out, what came naturally to me helped me to keep the person I was interviewing more comfortable, and I got more time and substance from the interview as a result. I didn't have to approach the ambush execution-style, the way I'd seen other reporters do it on the news. I learned to trust my unique approach. I'm wired as a people-pleaser and my wiring was enough to get what I was after.

Look at the people who stand out as great successes in the world. You'll see one after another did things differently than other people did them. Maybe it's because it was the only way they could, but they owned it. That's bold.

Questions to Ponder:

What is something unique about you?

How can you use your unique qualities to support yourself professionally? personally?

#3. Know Your People

Engage the People Around You

Really knowing the people you do life with lends itself to stronger relationships and community. The stronger the relationship we have with someone, the safer we feel to be our authentic selves.

Years ago my longtime friend, Elle Zimmerman, offered to give me the group Enneagram session that she puts on for businesses across the country as a certified Enneagram coach. I invited my daughter and nieces to take part in the session. By the end of our roundtable discussion, I understood these precious young women better than I ever thought possible. What drives them. Why they react the way they do to things and situations. How to best encourage them. Likewise, they understand me better. Why I say and do the things the way I say and do them. It forever strengthened the bonds between us.

As I've said throughout this book, relationships are everything. Valuing someone enough to get to know them doesn't just make them feel good. It offers you an opportunity to learn things that could be beneficial to you as well. As a business manager, this is gold.

One of my favorite examples involves the relationship between Mother Teresa and the woman who would someday replace her as the head of the Missionaries of Charity. Born into a devout Hindu family, Sister Nirmala Joshi went to see Mother Teresa at age 17 upon hearing about her work. Mother Teresa didn't just welcome her, she got to know her and learned Sister Nirmala had previously studied law. Soon after Sister Nirmala joined the Missionaries of Charity as a Catholic nun, Mother Teresa sent her to the University of Calcutta to get her law degree. She then sent Sister Nirmala out to set up new homes for the sick and poor around the world.[14] You can see how Mother Teresa managed to get her Missionaries of Charity into 123 countries by the time of her death. She was intentional in getting to know her people and that enabled her to place her people in the right positions for the growth of her organization.

Establish a Board of Directors

I've referred to my inner circle of girlfriends as my Board of Directors. This is a concept borrowed from Napoleon Hill, author of the longtime bestseller "Think and Grow Rich," who spoke of regularly meeting with a "Master Mind group."[15] Actually, I have some men on my "board" too. These are people I trust, because they are wise, they really know me, and they trust me enough to give me truth. Having these kinds of connections is critical in building boldness.

People will say all manner of things to you and about you. You'll be praised and you'll be criticized. Sometimes it's hard to know whom to believe. You need to know the truth about how you show up in the world, so that you can be confident in your strengths, overcome your shortcomings, and discount certain opinions about you. Those people who know you and will tell you the truth can help you to navigate this. Know who they are, ask them for feedback, and trust it.

Questions to Ponder:

How do you invest in your current relationships?

What is one way you can invest in building new relationships?

Who is on your Board of Directors? If you don't have one, whom could you ask to be your trusted advisors?

#4. Know Your Business

Do Your Homework

Before I walked into interviews surrounding big investigations as a reporter, I made outlines and arranged my notes in a way that I could get to information quickly and remember everything I was going to need to ask. My preparation became more elaborate over time because I had learned from previous interviews what more I needed to do in order to better prepare. In the latter years of my career, I was on fire in these interviews. It felt incredible to be so in command. In one of the most important interviews I did, I realized at the end that I hadn't even looked down at my notes. Amid the interview I had a natural instinct that I needed to keep eye contact with the person in order to keep the interview going.

Being fully prepared absolutely freed me to engage fully in this interview and to boldly ask the tough questions that were outside of my comfort zone. It was incredible! Nothing feels better than having done your homework. Your whole body feels different going into the big test, whether you're in school or out in the business world.

Doing detailed prep work is generally not the fun part of pursuing our passions, but we have to embrace it. How well you're prepared for what you're walking into will determine whether you're nervous and anxious or peaceful and confident. That affects how much boldness you can bring.

Questions to Ponder:

Do you need to do "homework" to know your business better?

What is one situation in which you can be better prepared? At work? In your personal life?

#5. Know When to Laugh

"Against the assault of laughter, nothing can stand." Mark Twain[16]

Find Your Sense of Humor

My dad had a regular go-to message for me growing up when I'd get down or otherwise overwhelmed about something. He'd remind me of what his dad, Gampa O'Neill, would always tell him. "Don't take yourself so seriously."

Gampa was a concert pianist. Daddy was an opera singer. We artists especially have an inclination to go deep and dark. So this one is especially for the hopelessly soulful or otherwise extreme types who have this tendency. Keeping your sense of humor will keep you going when the demons attack. Nothing good comes from losing your zest for life. Laughter heals. It's a scientific fact.

Feed Your Sense of Humor

For as long as I can remember, I've had a regular sitcom to watch at night while winding down. Cheers, Seinfeld, The Office… So many good ones. One of these days I'm going to send a thank you note to the writers of these shows who've gotten me through all manner of difficult moments in life.

I also have go-to friends and relatives who are hilariously funny. Brenna, Sherry, Cathy, Peggy, Alex… The list goes on. I find I'm drawn to funny people. Be in the company of people whose humor lifts you to "happy."

We have to feed ourselves what we need and we human beings need humor.

Use Your Sense of Humor

Remember Merv's practical joke from Chapter 4? Merv was the master! He knew how to use humor to put people at ease. It made him a great interviewer back in his day, and my time with him made me a better interviewer in the future.

Humor is tricky. People respond differently to different kinds of humor, but try to infuse it where you can. The more we are at ease with ourselves, the bolder we can be.

Questions to Ponder:

Who are the people in your life that make you laugh?

Can you identify the things that make you laugh?

———————◇———————

As WWII vet Charlie Geraci shared with us in Chapter 9, "Life is an experience. It's a happy experience if you look at it the right way." It's in that spirit that I've shared with you what's meant the difference on my path in life.

Thank you for the opportunity to share with you. Good luck and Godspeed as you cross the footbridge to know your boldness!

NOTES

Chapter 2: KATY BAR THE DOOR
How I "Broke Into" Broadcast News

1   *Merriam-Webster* (2023, February 7). The definition of bold. https://www.merriam-webster.com/dictionary/bold
2   Jacobs Hendel, Hilary (2016). The Role of Make Believe Play in Adult Life. *PsychCentral*. https://psychcentral.com/blog/the-role-of-make-believe-play-in-adult-life#1

Chapter 4: THE NERVE OF MERV
The Media Giant's Practical Joke

3   Severo, Richard and Wyatt, Edward (2007). Merv Griffin, Television Innovator, Dies at 82. *New York Times*. https://www.nytimes.com/2007/08/13/arts/television/13griffin.html The New York Times

Chapter 5: TIME TO THROW A HAIL MARY
My Interview with a Saint

4   Wilding, Melody (2022, March 10). How to Stop Overthinking and Start Trusting Your Gut. *Harvard Business Review*. https://hbr.org/2022/03/how-to-stop-overthinking-and-start-trusting-your-gut
5   Vardey, Linda (compiled by) (1995). *Mother Teresa: A Simple Path*.
6   Mother Teresa and Kolodiejchuk, Brian, *Come Be My Light: The Private Writings of the Saint of Calcutta*, New York: Crown Publishing Group (2007).
7   Missionaries of Charity (2023) https://missionariesofcharity.org/our-history-read-more.html

[8] Joshi, Vijay (1998, April 12). A Home For Suffering Iraqi Children -- Mother Teresa's Order Helps Handicapped, Ill. *The Seattle Times* https://archive.seattletimes. com/archive/?date=19980412&slug=2744785

Chapter 7: WELCOME TO THE BIG SHOW
How do you like me now?

[9] Marcus Allen Claims Simpson Asked Him to Lie (1996, May 31) *CNN* http://www.cnn.com/US/9605/31/simpson/

[10] Resnick, Faye and Walker, Mike (October 1, 1994). *Nicole Brown Simpson: The Private Diary of a Life Interrupted*. Dove Books.

Chapter 8: HOME ALONE WITH A KILLER
Canvassing a Neighborhood Could Prove Fatal

[11] (2013, May 23) Merit Brief of Plaintiff-Appellee, State of Ohio. *Clerk of Court. Supreme Court of Ohio.* https://www.supremecourt.ohio.gov/pdf_viewer/pdf_viewer.aspx?pdf=727862.pdf&subdirectory=2012-0405\DocketItems&source=DL_Clerk

Chapter 10: THE OVER AND UNDER ON SURVIVING
What are the Odds I'll Outlast This One?

[12] Keith, Kent M. *Anyway: The Paradoxical Commandments (2023)* https://www.paradoxicalcommandments.com/motherteresaconnection

Chapter 11: DON'T ROCK THE BOAT, BABY
Will We Sink or Swim?

[13] Zimmer, Ben (2009, July 18). Was Cronkite Really the First "Anchorman?" *Slate.* https://slate.com/news-and-politics/2009/07/was-cronkite-really-the-first-anchorman.html

Chapter 14: YOUR PATH FORWARD
5 Stepping Stones on the Footbridge to Bold

[14] Mattei, Giampaolo (1998, August 5) Sr. Nirmala Joshi of the Missionaries of Charity. *L'Osservatore Romano.* https://www.ewtn.com/catholicism/library/sr-nirmala-joshi-of-the-missionaries-of-charity-9179

[15] Hill, Napoleon, *Think and Grow Rich.* p.154, Gildan Media LLC. (2019) (originally published 1937)

[16] The Mysterious Stranger. Twain, Mark. Published by Harper & Brothers, Publishers, New York and London, 1916.

ACKNOWLEDGEMENTS

Behind every bold woman stands a team of advisors, encouragers, and givers of all kinds.

From the bottom of my heart, I would like to thank...

My best friend and executive producer on this project, Elle Zimmerman, who has patiently and tirelessly provided me with her professional expertise to guide me through every step of envisioning, writing, publishing and promoting this book.

My friends and mentors, who served as advisors willing to weigh in on what I share in this book, namely:

Brenna Kennedy, Cathy Sonne, Christi Cornette, Toni Cardinal, Marsanne Golsby, George Sells, Laurie Linehan, Brendan Linehan, Darielle Linehan, Peggy O'Neill, Curtis Zimmerman, G. Mitchell Ballard, and Randy Freking.

My family members who've encouraged me to boldly pursue my passion, who've always encouraged me on my path, and who've lifted me up along the way, especially: Mom, Alex, Raph, Peggy, Laurie, Brendan, Audrey, Emily, Ryan, Marston, Maxwell, Liam, Grace, Griffin, Aunt Patt, Aunt Gerri, Uncle Kenny, Pete, Ricky, Steve, Uncle Brigham, Aunt Bette, Jimmy, Stevie, Heather, Josie, Uncle Don, Aunt Gwen, and Trevor.

The O'Neill family (Christmas, 2016)

My Bold Ambassadors, the many friends who believed in this project and stepped up to cheer me on as they spread the word, especially the Elder Warriors of the Green Berets who've always assured me they have my back.

And last, but certainly not least…

My Heavenly Father, his Son, and the Holy Spirit who brought me peace and joy throughout this journey.

ABOUT THE AUTHOR

Julie O'Neill is a speaker, author, and former news anchor, whose dynamic personality has entertained since her first stint in live television at age 6 on the "O'Neill Family Christmas Show." Her work in TV news has been seen on ABC, CBS, CNN, and local stations across the country, and included interviews with a president, a saint, and CEOs of multi-billion dollar companies.

Julie's quick wit and keen insights have inspired and captivated audiences of top business executives, spiritual leaders, supporters of nonprofits and students of all ages. Her humor, charisma and contagious laugh make her a favorite emcee and keynote speaker.

A singer in her spare time, Julie has performed the National Anthem for countless events, including a Cincinnati Reds home game and the inaugural ceremony of the World Peace Bell. (She also does a pretty good Shania Twain!)

She is a proud mother of two and dog Blue, living in Loveland, Ohio.

To bring Julie to your next event, contact her at:
JulieONeillSpeaks.com
Email: julie@JulieONeillSpeaks.com
Facebook: Julie O'Neill
Linkedin: Julie O'Neill

.

Made in USA - Kendallville, IN
30494_9798987663806
06.06.2023 1340